D0710091

IF YOU LIKE
MONTY
PYTHON...

IF YOU LIKE

MONTY PYTHON...

HERE ARE OVER 200 MOVIES,
TV SHOWS, AND OTHER ODDITIES
THAT YOU WILL LOVE

ZACK HANDLEN

AN IMPRINT OF HAL LEONARD CORPORATION

Published in 2012 by Limelight Editions
An Imprint of Hal Leonard Corporation
7777 West Bluemound Road
Milwaukee, WI 53213

Trade Book Division Editorial Offices
33 Plymouth St., Montclair, NJ 07042

Printed in the United States of America

Book design by Michael Kellner

Library of Congress Cataloging-in-Publication Data

Handlen, Zack.
  If you like Monty Python : here are over 200 movies, tv shows, and other oddities that you will love / Zack Handlen. -- 1st paperback ed.
     p. cm.
  Includes index.
  ISBN 978-0-87910-393-4
  1. Monty Python (Comedy troupe) 2. Monty Python's flying circus (Television program) 3. Comedy films--Miscellanea. 4. Television comedies--Miscellanea.
I. Title.
  PN2599.5.T54H36 2012
  791.43'617--dc23
                                        2011047192

www.limelighteditions.com

For Ally

CONTENTS

Preface

It's simple: there's a finite supply of Monty Python in the
world. And once you've finished going through that supply—once
you've watched the entire run of *Monty Python's Flying Circus*, seen
each of the four movies a dozen times over, wasted hours reciting
dialogue and gags to your like-minded friends, played the computer games, even played the short-lived collectible card game—well,
what happens next? Great art of any kind should be satisfying, but
it rarely feels like enough, especially not when the art in question is
some of the greatest comedy ever put to screen.

So, once you've exhausted the work of Graham Chapman, John
Cleese, Terry Gilliam, Eric Idle, Terry Jones, and Michael Palin, it's
time to try something new. To that end, we've constructed the book
you now hold in your hands. *If You Like Monty Python* aims to give
the erstwhile Pythonite a map forward through the confusing territory. In the following chapters (separated by general subject and/
or medium), you'll find suggested additional material that should
keep you busy watching, listening, reading, and laughing for however long it takes science to write a program that will give us more
Python sketches.

This is not intended as a definitive list of, well, anything. Nor is
it a history of the troupe, nor a precisely calculated lineup of every
comedian, writer, or lunatic who ever claimed to be influenced by
the Superlative Six. Think of it, instead, as a collection of new di-
rections, with the hope that some few may lead you, the reader, to
other, equally fervent fandoms. Who knows—maybe buried here

is the name of an artist who will affect you so powerfully that in some not-so-distant future, you'll find yourself writing about them in a book much like this one. And then you'll show us. You'll show us all!

Anyway. Video stores are scarce these days, and condescending-yet-instructive video store clerks are still scarcer, so consider us your assistant in the process of selecting an evening's entertainment. The only drawback being, there are 200 or so items mentioned in this volume, and you'll probably work through all of those eventually, much as you did with Python's oeuvre, given your apparently insatiable lust for killing time. But if that does happen, well, you'll be dead anyway soon enough, so maybe you should consider going outside for a walk or something, before someone nails you to a tree. Always look on the bright side, that's what we say.

NOTE: In America, different years of a television show are called "seasons." In Britain, different years of a television show are called "series." Throughout this book, I've endeavored to refer to each show by the nomenclature of its homeland.

Author's Note: Throughout this book, certain names and titles have been listed in boldface. This occurs only at the first, or primary, reference to each item, and this is done to indicate that the name or title is considered essential.

Chico, Groucho, and Harpo of the Marx Brothers. (Photofest)

1

BEFORE THERE WAS PYTHON, THERE WAS...

Monty Python didn't come into this world without some precedent. The troupe is as much a summation of what came before it as it is a statement of purpose for the future. In the following chapter are a number of movies, shows, and other potential Python influences. These have been arranged in rough chronology.

The art of Charlie Chaplin is undoubtedly a key piece in the history of comedy and the history of cinema. His best films are required viewing for any student of the medium, but Chaplin isn't necessarily suited to the Python sensibility. The actor/director/writer's innovative approach to story-telling, his brilliant composed comic set pieces, and his strong visual style have all aged well, but his sentimentality is a trickier case, effective for some, distracting for others. Pythonites in particular may not take to it, as any sweetness in the Monty Python canon is difficult to find and nearly always quickly undercut.

Which isn't to say that appreciation of one contradicts the potential for appreciation of the other. A devoted fan of Monty Python should be a devoted fan of the art of comedy in general, and that means cultivating an appreciation for the best of the genre. Those Pythonites looking for a good entry point into Chaplin would do well to check out ***Modern Times*** (1936), Chaplin's goofy satire of the perils and potential of living in the modern world. The Little Tramp suffers the indignity of life on the factory assembly line, loses his job due to his unfortunate predilection for destructive slapstick, and finds true love with a young woman played by Paulette Goddard. Less a plotted movie than a series of vignettes strung together by character, *Times* has some of Chaplin's most famous set pieces, including his trip through oversized gears in the bowels of a machine, and the Tramp's only spoken words, a nonsense song sung in pseudo-French. Goddard is remarkable, and while Chaplin's shtick may not work for everyone, his physical grace and talent for slapstick are still a marvel.

Any Pythonite interested in the height of silent comedy without all the heart would do well to check out the films of Buster Keaton. Working in roughly the same era as Chaplin, Keaton also wrote, directed, and starred in his own best pictures. Where Chaplin's best known character, the Tramp, could be readily identified by a buoyant spirit and boundless optimism, Keaton's on-screen persona is far more pragmatic, a stoic, ever-patient victim of the world's absurdities. Where the Tramp would smile, a Keaton hero stares, stone-faced, at the challenges before him, but that unsmiling visage never reads as uncaring or cold. Rather, its humanism shines through: resignation, and a refusal to surrender to chance.

Keaton's two best films, **The General** (1927) and **Sherlock, Jr.** (1924), test that refusal considerably. In *The General*, Keaton plays a railway engineer in the South at the start of the Civil War. When Keaton's attempts to enlist are refused due to his value as a railroad worker, he's branded a coward by the family of the girl he loves. He gets a chance to prove himself a year later, when Union spies steal his beloved train, and his beloved, and he embarks on an epic quest to win her back. The scope and scale of the stunt gags in *The General* remain a marvel even today, as Keaton dangles from train cars, dodges cannon fire, and blows up bridges with aplomb. The adventure holds up as well, and represents a high-water mark for silent film storytelling.

Shorter than *The General*, but even more remarkable in its playful inventiveness, *Sherlock, Jr.* features a movie theater projectionist (Keaton) with ambitions towards being the world's greatest detective, as well as winning the girl next door. But that girl's suitor has other ideas, and frames Keaton for the theft of his beloved's precious pocket watch. Despondent, Keaton returns to the theater, where he dreams himself into the movie on-screen as the ever-resourceful Sherlock, Jr. *Sherlock* dazzles with its rapid-fire pace and remarkable imaginative gifts, as Keaton interacts with a movie screen in ways that still impress even today. Chaplin may be better known, but Keaton is arguably closer to the Python heart: trapped in a cold, nonsensical world, where the only escape is a quick mind and quicker feet.

It would be impossible to imagine modern comedy without taking Monty Python into account. The same could easily be said for the **Marx Brothers**, a family of American comedians whose anarchic, vaudevillian wit influenced generations of writers and performers. Groucho, Chico, and Harpo remain indelibly imprinted on the American psyche: the smart-ass with glasses and a shoe-polish mustache; the devious, thick-accented foreigner looking to work the system; and the silent, horn-honking child. (The two younger Marx brothers, Gummo and Zeppo, failed to make the same impression, although Zeppo did appear in the group's first five movies.) It would be easy enough to fill an entire book, much like this one, with all the various shows and movies that the Marxes helped inspire. The brothers made a total of thirteen films together, and while not all of them work as well as the others, their legacy remains.

The best way to appreciate the Marxes is probably by watching their greatest movie, ***Duck Soup*** (1933). There's trouble in far-off Freedonia—the coffers are empty, and hope is in short supply. The wealthy dowager Mrs. Teasdale (Margaret Dumont, a foil for the Marx brothers who appeared in seven of their movies) has agreed to offer financial aid, but only if Rufus T. Firefly (Groucho) is appointed leader of the country. Firefly arrives, but seems less interested in solving the country's problems and more interested in avoiding work and wooing Teasdale. While he gets cigar ash over everything, the neighboring country of Sylvania is plotting to take advantage of Freedonia's impoverished state. To that end, Ambassador Trentino (Louis Calhern) hires Chicolini (Chico) and Pinky (Harpo) to spy on Firefly.

Other Marx Brothers movies would have more of a plot—the story here works as passable satire of the absurdity of war, but the movie is best regarded as a pure, unadulterated shot of comic calamity. At sixty-eight minutes, *Soup* contains not an ounce of fat, and the film has some of the brothers' best gags, including, most famously, the mirror sketch, in which Harpo matches an increasingly impressed Groucho move for move. Groucho and the others stuck to playing themselves from movie to movie, so any film in their filmography is bound to have something worth watching. ***A Night at the Opera*** (1935) would be a good place to go next, as it represents a more conventional style of film comedy for the brothers that would largely define the rest of their careers. But for the pure stuff, *Duck Soup* can't be beat. It's the wild, anything-for-a-laugh approach that will be familiar to Pythonites—life may be a cruel joke, but at least it's a funny one.

Class was always a major satirical target for the Pythons; the distinctions between lords and commoners, combined with the characteristic British distaste for direct conversation, were often a source for the troupe's best sketches. Plenty of other British comedies mined this material, but none better than the 1949 Ealing Studios film ***Kind Hearts and Coronets***. Dennis Price stars as Louis Mazzini, the outcast son of the D'Ascoyne family, who determines to murder his way into inheriting the D'Ascoyne dukedom of Chalfont. Alec Guinness plays the family members who stand in Price's way (including one woman), and Joan Greenwood and Valerie Hobson costar as the women who help drive Price to such great heights.

Guinness's tour-de-force performance usually gets the most praise, and that's well deserved. Without ever being showy or calling attention to himself, the actor manages to give each individual D'Ascoyne a clear, recognizable personality. But Price is even more crucial to the film's success. His calm, perfectly polite demeanor conceals a blinding rage at the wrongs he feels have been done to him. That demeanor sets the tone of the film: chipper, impeccable, and utterly acidic. *Coronets* is more reserved than Python, but it shares the troupe's understanding of the essential absurdity of the class system. Supplanting decency with etiquette leads to monsters with all the right smiles.

Guinness would make other movies with Ealing, and while none quite hit *Coronets'* acidic perfection, most remain classics in their own right and an excellent picture of British comedy of the time. Of these other films, ***The Ladykillers*** (1955) comes the closest to the black comedy sweet spot of *Coronets*. Guinness stars as Professor Marcus, a criminal mastermind who rents out a room for the purposes of planning a major bank robbery with the aid of a gang of hardened criminals. Unfortunately for Marcus and his gang, the room he picks is in the home of Mrs. Louisa Alexandra Wilberforce (Katie Johnson), a sweet, trusting, good-natured elderly woman who nonetheless represents the end of all of Marcus's hopes and nefarious plotting.

The Ladykillers is an oddity. While *Coronets* depicted murder as a sort of gentleman's art, the series of deaths, accidental and otherwise, that take out Marcus and his cohorts are played for broader laughs, and the gang members themselves are cartoonish caricatures. Which isn't to say they aren't effective caricatures—*Ladykillers* features Herbert Lom and Peter Sellers (in one of his first film roles), as well as Danny Green and Cecil Parker, and all manage to paint quick but clear portraits of nefarious men thoroughly out of their depth in the face of someone who reminds them of their mums. Guinness uses prop teeth and stringy white hair to create a simultaneously threatening and ridiculous villain, and Johnson is convincingly pleasant as the heart of all the chaos.

The Man in the White Suit (1951) is far more genial than either *Ladykillers* or *Coronets*. Guinness plays Sidney Stratton, a young chemist who develops a new form of fabric that never gets dirty and never wears out. He decides it's his duty to bring this cloth to the masses, but runs into some resistance from both cloth manufacturers and the trade unions that represent those who work for cloth manufacturers. The problem is that Sidney's invention will eventually render the production of new clothing, if not obsolete, than at the very least severely curtailed.

White Suit isn't as riotously funny as *Ladykillers* or as acidic as *Coronets*, but it is a fascinating, thoughtful examination of what might happen if someone actually did invent the proverbial better mousetrap. As Sidney, Guinness is guileless, charming, and utterly incapable of understanding why his brilliance is causing so many problems, and Joan Greenwood, as a sympathetic mill owner's daughter, plays a far better-natured leading lady than her turn in *Coronets*. A science fiction film that plays largely as light comedy, *White Suit* raises issues that are still relevant today about the relationship between progress and labor, and the nature of science to pursue its own ends, regardless of social effect.

Finally, there's **The Lavender Hill Mob** (1951). Here, Guinness plays Henry Holland, a shy bank clerk who uses his position and general unobtrusiveness to plot and carry out the theft of a load of gold bullion. Where *Ladykillers* and *Coronets* played off murder and black farce, and *White Suit* had serious commentary on social conditions underlying its fantasy, *Hill Mob* is as genial as its hero, a pleasant, somewhat-lighter-than-air confection of crime and foolishness. The film suffers slightly from an overly moralistic ending that takes a bit of fun out of the proceedings. It lacks the bite of Guinness's other major Ealing comedies, but it's still worth watching as an overall delightful lark, and as a reminder that even the meekest of men have the potential for great mischief.

When Charles Schulz's small-scale epic **Peanuts** (1950–2000) debuted in newspapers on October 2, 1950, it looked a little different from what would come to be arguably the most famous newspaper comic strip of all time. Snoopy didn't belong to Charlie Brown; Linus didn't exist yet; and other characters would be gradually phased out of the limelight over the months and years to make way for soon-to-be familiar faces. (Schulz didn't even much care for the name "Peanuts.") But Charlie Brown was there. Good ole lovable blockheaded Charlie Brown, the most likable loser in popular fiction, the guy who always got picked last, got forgotten, and never got any Valentine's Day cards. Which meant that the core value of the strip was already in place—characters lost. Often and repeatedly, and with no end in sight.

Over the next fifty years, Charles Schulz assembled his main cast (loudmouthed, selfish Lucy; her saintly, shy younger brother Linus; Charlie's little sister Sally; the piano-playing Schroeder; the athletic romantic foil Peppermint Patty; and so on), but that loser's aesthetic remained firmly in place. It's an aesthetic the strips share with Python's two best movies, *Monty Python and the Holy Grail* and *Life of Brian*, both of which feature heroes forever struggling to achieve that which is perpetually beyond their grasp. Python generally went for a more overtly silly feel with its stories of eternal defeat, but there are moments in *Brian* especially that share *Peanuts'* profound melancholy, and the understanding that wanting to be accepted and loved isn't the same thing is knowing how to achieve either.

Really, though, *Peanuts* is entirely its own construction, a gag-a-day newspaper strip that managed to work within the dictates of its medium to tell its stories without ever drawing that much attention to itself. Schulz's work found its way into books, television specials (**A Charlie Brown Christmas** (1965), the first *Peanuts* animated show, is one of the best Christmas specials ever made), movies, and even the occasional ad, and not all of it was high quality. In his final years, Schulz's writing lost much of the snap of his best work. but the characters remained iconic, and the entire run of the strip remains one of the strongest long-form pieces of fiction ever created. In *Peanuts*, there were few victories, but there was humor to be had in the art of failure, and a deep compassion for anyone who's ever hoped desperately for a certain moment—only to end up flat on his back, staring up at the sky. Fantagraphics is currently in the process of reprinting the entire series, in books that cover two years apiece, with the final volume due in 2016.

It's a sad fact of life that art—especially popular entertainment—doesn't always age well. Sometimes it's references that become stale, names of famous fools and cultural landmarks slipping through the cracks of long decades. Sometimes whole styles can fall out favor, become either too predictable or too offensive to be sustained. And sometimes, tastes simply change, and what used to be funny or exciting just becomes odd. The test of a truly great work is its ability to weather these currents in ways that no one creator can predict.

The Goon Show (1951–1960), the classic BBC Home Service radio program that helped launch the careers of Peter Sellers and Spike Milligan, has suffered a little from the ravages of time. The show recorded in front of a live studio audience, and while the audience laughter works to the show's advantage, punctuating gags and adding to the performers' energy, there are times when the audience's reaction to a seemingly innocent line indicates a point of common reference that is no longer so common. What's impressive, then, is how well the show holds up regardless. It's so good, in fact, that you may find yourself laughing along to even the jokes you *don't* get.

A number of members of Monty Python have cited *The Goon Show* as one of their formative influences, and listening to the show now, it's not hard to see why. Running over 238 episodes all told, the show had a variety of formats, but in its most consistent form, each episode would center on a single story, featuring some of the show's recurring characters, which were performed by Milligan, Sellers, and Harry Secombe. (Secombe was a replacement for Michael Bentine, who left in 1953). As creator of the series and the writer most responsible for its tone and content, Milligan brought comedy to the radio in a way that remains fresh even now. Police officers tracked down the batter pudding hurlers, English football teams squared off against the hordes of Caesar, and all manner of silliness.

That's crucial to note, actually. *The Goon Show* is a wonderful, cheerfully silly show, not in a leering, *Benny Hill* fashion (leering is difficult on the radio, requiring special microphones), but with all the childish glee of smart kids running amok. That silliness would go on to infect Python members in much same way the snotty sarcasm of *Beyond the Fringe* informed their point of view; the Goons used puns, linguistic absurdities, clever syllogisms, surreal connections, goofy voices, and suggested slapstick, with a rampant glee. It's not at all difficult to imagine a young Cleese or Palin hearing the program and getting the inspiration for an entire career. Milligan and company were men who made a living out of mocking anything that wasn't tied down, and even much of what was. And while the occasional name may fly over modern heads, the absurdity remains universal.

The Rocky & Bullwinkle Show (1959–1964) is an animated children's program about, among other things, a talking flying squirrel named Rocket "Rocky" J. Squirrel, and his closet pal, the sweet but dimwitted Bullwinkle J. Moose. Anyone raised on the modern animation of kid classics like *Batman: The Animated Series* or *Tiny Toon Adventures* may be shocked to see that the animation quality of the *R & B Show* is . . . less than good. It's hideous, in fact. Characters don't so much move as jerk from place to place, proportions never match up the way they should, and the human characters, like the villainous Boris Badenov, look human only because they couldn't possibly be anything else. But whether the animation quality is intentional or not, it's part of the show's undeniable charm. *R & B* is a goofy, goony, big-hearted show where no pun is too painful, and no punch line too broad. It's a show for kids, so maybe that's why it looks a bit sloppy—*kids* are a bit sloppy.

Besides, *R & B* plays as much like an illustrated radio show as anything else, a televised *Goon Show* that follows the Goons' love of broad gags and silliness injected into pulp adventure stories. Each episode of the five-season show (which started life as *Rocky and His Friends*, before changing its title to *The Bullwinkle Show* in 1961), follows Rocky and Bullwinkle as they travel the world, thwart evil schemes, and evade the constant threat of sudden death. Their stories generally unfold over multiple episodes, with each episode featuring two installments of the ongoing tale. In between their stories, there are segments about Dudley Do-Right, a stalwart Canadian Mountie fighting against the evil Snidely Whiplash; "Fractured Fairy Tales," which retell classic stories like "Little Red Riding Hood" and "The Sleeping Beauty" with a modern spin; and "Peabody's Improbable History," about a talking dog, his pet boy Sherman, and a time machine.

Rocky and Bullwinkle's serialized adventures are often surprisingly complex, and while the show isn't exactly suspenseful or gripping, its genial, anything-for-a-laugh tone covers writing sophisticated enough to satisfy children *and* adults. One of the first animated programs to prove it was possible to entertain all ages without insulting any of them, the show, created by Jay Ward, Alex Anderson and Bill Scott, still has plenty of snap to it, and Pythonites will appreciate its low-key wit and riffs on all sorts of cultural history, while overlooking its less-than-cutting-edge appearance. Besides, it's not like fans of *Flying Circus*, with its frequent cut-and-paste interludes by Terry Gilliam, are unfamiliar with animation more interested in ideas than presentation.

In its most basic form, a comedy sketch has two players: the funny man and the straight man. The funny man will introduce the sketch's concept, and do most of the work sustaining that concept, while the straight man reacts to the concept, generally growing increasingly irritated as the situation becomes more complicated. In the majority of Monty Python sketches that featured just two performers (like the Dead Parrot sketch), the troupe would follow this form, but the straight man would be just as loony as the funny one. As a stand-up comedian, **Bob Newhart** ran a solo sketch act. He served as the straight man *and* as the funny one, and the results were hugely successful.

In horror, the most frightening monster is often the one that remains unseen, forcing the audience to imagine something far worse than anything that could be shown on screen. Newhart's style operates on the same principle, only putting laughter in the place of screams. Take "Driving Instructor," a track off Newhart's debut album, ***The Button-Down Mind of Bob Newhart*** (1960). Newhart enacts a scene of a justifiably nervous driving instructor giving a lesson to a woman he calls "Mrs. Webb." Mrs. Webb never speaks, but it's possible to deduce her half of the conversation, as well as the catastrophic drive she takes her instructor on, from Newhart's stuttering, ingratiating responses.

The effect is that an already pretty good gag (Mrs. Webb is a terrible driver, and Newhart's unnamed instructor has no idea what he's in for) becomes exponentially more effective, as well as, in its own modest way, surprisingly innovative. Newhart would go on to make his name as a television star, most notably on the sitcoms **The Bob Newhart Show** (1972–1978) and **Newhart** (1982–1990), but his early albums are probably of the most interest to Pythonites. *Button-Down Mind*, **The Button-Down Mind Strikes Back** (1961), **Behind the Button-Down Mind of Bob Newhart** (1961), and **The Button-Down Mind on TV** (1962) are all excellent. Anyone looking for a collection of Newhart's best routines could also check out 2001's **Something Like This ... The Bob Newhart Anthology.** Other stand-ups from Newhart's era recorded work that hasn't held up nearly as well, but Newhart's style makes his routines universal and unique: a nice man, struggling to maintain composure in the face of a maddening world.

Monty Python never acted cool. Which is not to say that they *weren't* cool. While fervent knowledge of the group's routines has become a calling card of nerdery the world over, it seems reasonable enough to assume that the group members themselves were pretty darn hip, considering the popularity of their television series. But Palin et al. never *acted* cool, because acting cool is as quick a way to kill comedy as not bothering to include jokes. *Flying Circus* required its cast to adopt silly voices, mince about like loons, wear women's clothing, and, in general, be as utterly uncool as was possible. But it stands to reason that the devoted Pythonite might want a glimpse of the height of cool humor before the troupe came on the scene, and with that in mind, we suggest a look at **The Avengers** (1961–1969), for an example of the epitome of British cool.

A sly spy thriller with a healthy awareness of its campy underpinnings, *The Avengers* stars Patrick Macnee as John Steed, a gentleman's gentleman with a deep sense of a style and a deeper commitment to defending Her Majesty and the realm against the forces of evil. The series went through a number of growing pains in its early years, but the form it's best remembered for today (and the one that shows *Avengers* at its best) teams Steed up with a young woman in his quest for justice, first Honor Blackman (who played Pussy Galore in *Goldfinger*), then Diana Rigg, and finally Linda Thorson. In each hour-long episode, the duo would learn of a nefarious plot against their government, and it would be up to quick thinking and a smart application of fisticuffs and kung-fu to save the day. The show set its tone in the opening credits: a nearly bare set, a jazzy score, and Macnee's simple "We're needed," and it was off to the races, and, eventually, a nice cup of tea.

The Avengers had it all: great costume design, smart writing, and terrific chemistry between its two leads, most particularly when Diana Rigg was on the show. She and Macnee exchanged sly double entendres with the light touch of skilled tennis players at the match. As Emma Peel, Rigg is the epitome of the cultured, thinking man's sex symbol, and, somewhat unusually for the era, she often engaged in hand-to-hand combat as well as devastating verbal put-downs. In a sense, Steed, with his bowler hats and old-school style, represented a part of what Monty Python, in all its terrible silliness, was revolting against: the old guard who refused to give ground even as they lost relevancy in the modern world. Still, it's hard to deny Macnee's charm, or Rigg's timeless charisma. Other shows would risk more in their writing, but few would match *The Avengers'* leads for panache.

Flying Circus was a revolution, but revolutions rarely arrive without antecedents. Much of the '60s in British entertainment was a slow build towards an environment in which the Pythons could thrive, and arguably the opening shot of the war was fired in **Beyond the Fringe**. A theater revue that opened in Edinburgh in 1960, *Fringe* starred Jonathan Miller, Dudley Moore, Peter Cook, and Alan Bennett in a series of satirical sketches, many of which lampooned prominent British authority figures. The show ran with its original cast till 1964, and exists today as an album and a DVD recording of a show from their 1964 revival run.

Viewed today, it isn't immediately apparent what made *Fringe* so hugely influential in its time. Part of the reason the show is considered so important is its snide take on some of the most powerful men in Britain, including Peter Cook's impersonation of then Prime Minister Harold Macmillan. These days, those caricatures aren't nearly as effective, as they come off as generic stuffy authority figures behaving foolishly. Yet the performances and writing are strong enough that the reasons behind the show's impact become clear over time. In particular, *Fringe*'s blend of surreal madness with stiff-upper-lip English decorum is a major recurring theme in *Flying Circus*, which shared this show's disregard for the powerful—and its grasp of how the absurd can undermine that power handily.

Which isn't to say the show doesn't work in its own right. While the topical humor may not always land, the majority of *Fringe* is given over to schoolboy snickering and timeless sketch concepts. Of particulate note is "One Leg Too Few," in which a one-legged Dudley Moore auditions to Peter Cook for the role of Tarzan; "The Great Train Robbery," in which Cook explains police procedure in the wake of a railway-related theft; and "The Aftermyth of the War," which charts Britain's involvement in World War II in a largely unserious fashion. *Fringe* is required viewing for Pythonites, and for anyone interested in the history of British comedy.

These days, it's easy to take for granted that television shows stick around. Unless a series is canceled after a few episodes, it'll live on after it airs in reruns, online, and on DVD. But it wasn't always this way. Peter Cook and Dudley Moore's sketch comedy program *Not Only . . . But Also* ran for three series in the 1960s, for a total of twenty-four episodes (including a Christmas special in 1966), but when the BBC did a wipe of its videotaped programs, much of this material was lost. ***The Best of ... What's Left of ... Not Only ... But Also*** (1964–1970) is a collection of material taken from what's left of the show, edited together into six half-hour-long "episodes." This still leaves a far amount of existing material unreleased on DVD, but it's better than nothing.

Quite a bit better than nothing, in fact. Unlike *Flying Circus*, the sketches on *Not Only* are self-contained; despite the hodgepodge nature of the compilation, each new "episode" flows fairly well between character pieces, concept bits, and musical performances. The music is fun and the sketch material is as consistent as one would hope for, given the truncated nature of the source. *Best of ...* doesn't feel complete, exactly, but as a greatest-hits collection, it works well and is worth the time of Pythonites curious as to the state of British sketch comedy before *Flying Circus* hit the airwaves.

Not Only ... was originally meant as a solo outing for Dudley Moore, but, uncertain if he could carry a show by himself, Moore brought in Cook, whom he'd worked with on *Beyond the Fringe*. It's a good thing he did, as the interplay between the two is the show's greatest strength. Sketches were filmed live, in long takes, and many of them just serve as an excuse for the two performers to riff to each other on a concept or hook. Cook's dry, stoic approach bounces off Moore's more manic goofiness, and while it's a shame there's not more of the show, the two hours collected here are the product of a creative duo at the height of their powers.

It's possible to laugh about anything, but the scarier the subject, the gutsier a comedian needs to be to take advantage of it. You have to earn the right to laugh about the end of the world, but in ***Dr. Strangelove, or How I Learned to Stop Worrying and Love the Bomb*** (1964), director Stanley Kubrick finds a way to do just that. In a bleak, sharp satire about arguably the greatest of all national fears—the terror of the atomic bomb—Kubrick channels paranoia about the military, mistrust of authority, the absurdity of the patriarchy, and American/Russian relations. The resulting deadpan two-hour-long farce is a middle finger to anyone who ever embraced God and country without realizing they were holding nothing but air.

The story could've been played straight; the novel the screenplay is based on, *Red Alert* by Peter George, does exactly that. (It's been adapted into a non-comedic thriller multiple times, most famously as *Fail Safe*, starring Henry Fonda and Walter Matthau.) In *Strangelove*, the crazed General Jack D. Ripper (Sterling Hayden) sends a team of American bombers into Russia. With no way to contact the bombers, President Merkin Muffley (Peter Sellers) has to try and negotiate with the Russian premier to avoid disaster as he formulates a strategy with the advice of General Buck Turgidson (George C. Scott). Over Russia, pilot Major T. J. Kong (Slim Pickens) guides his men to perform the ultimate duty for their country, while back on the military base, Group Captain Lionel Mandrake (Peter Sellers, again) tries to bring reason to Ripper's mad plan. And in the situation room, Dr. Strangelove (Sellers, one more time) watches over all.

Plot alone doesn't convey the absurdity at work here. The performances are manic—Sellers gets the most attention, as his triple-role turn is an impressive piece of precision and commitment, but the whole cast is working at their peak. Scott transforms his typical gruff stoicism into a boyish ebullience that would be charming, if he weren't, y'know, talking about destroying hundreds of thousands of lives. Kubrick's clinical, detached style helps ground the wild performances, and the step-by-step approach showing how ridiculous people create catastrophes makes the absurdity as biting as it is entertaining.

Not all comedy about the possible end of the world has to be despairing. *Dr. Strangelove, or How I Learned to Stop Worrying and Love the Bomb* is a hilariously nihilistic look at the fevered egos, xenophobia, and frustrated lust that may someday doom us all, and **The Mouse That Roared** (1959) follows a somewhat similar path, with vastly different results. Both movies star Peter Sellers in three roles, and both films feature a magical, horrible, insanely destructive weapon that could singlehandedly change the course of global politics. But where *Strangelove* ends in conflagration and doom, *Mouse* has a far more optimistic take. It's the happiest world war film ever made.

Based on the 1955 novel of the same name by Leonard Wibberley, *Mouse* begins in Grand Fenwick, the smallest country in Europe, a dot on a dot on the map in the Alps. Fenwick's chief export is wine, but when an American winery starts producing a vintage that cuts into their profits, the Prime Minister of Fenwick (Peter Sellers) hits on a brilliant plan: Fenwick will declare war on the United States, and then immediately surrender, in order to take advantage of the U.S.'s generous postwar support. The Duchess of Fenwick (Sellers) approves of this plan, and the government sends an army of twenty, dressed in full armor and led by Tully Bascombe (Sellers), to New York to offer themselves to the police. Only, through a series of somewhat remarkable coincidences, Tully manages to get ahold of the insanely deadly Q bomb, the scientist who invented it, and the scientist's beautiful daughter (Jean Seberg), and, in doing so, wins the war he was supposed to lose.

Anyone looking for hard-hitting satire in *Mouse* will be disappointed; it's a sweet, occasionally adorable little movie where the worst thing to happen to anyone is an elevated stress level. The contrast between the subject (war, mass destruction, economic depression) and the tone is worth more than a few laughs, and Sellers is as reliable as ever in a triple-role turn that lacks the showiness of his *Strangelove* work but is effective nonetheless. Pythonites will enjoy the film's optimism, goofy charms, and the sight of Sellers in a wig.

Dr. Strangelove wasn't the only classic Peter Sellers comedy released in 1964. Sellers's most famous character, the hapless, bumbling Inspector Jacques Clouseau, debuted in 1963's *The Pink Panther*, but it wasn't until **A Shot in the Dark** that the character took center stage. Both films were directed by Blake Edwards, but where *Panther* was an elegant bedroom farce, *Shot* is something else entirely: a slapstick comedy of elegant, zany enthusiasm, and one of the truest expressions of Sellers's genius captured on film. Future sequels would dilute the Clouseau character into a pale shadow of his original self, but here, he's a fully realized creation of comic perfection.

This is especially impressive considering that the film is based on a stage play (*L'Idiote*) that doesn't feature the character at all. The movie (the screenplay was adapted by Edwards and William Peter Blatty of *Exorcist* fame) starts with the murder of Benjamin Ballon's (George Sanders) chauffeur, and all signs point to the maid, Maria (Elke Sommer), as the culprit. But when Clouseau is assigned the case, he immediately falls for Maria and is completely convinced of her innocence, despite the inconvenient habit members of Ballon's household staff have of dying whenever the maid is released from police custody. While Clouseau stumbles his way towards the real culprit, his boss, Commissioner Dreyfus (Herbert Lom), grows increasingly outraged over the inspector's path of inadvertent destruction, and all the while the real killer waits in the shadows . . .

Honestly, the mystery plot isn't really the draw here. *Shot*'s storyline is more of an excuse to hang a series of sketches together, from Clouseau's clumsy attempts at interrogation, to his even clumsier attempts at disguise, to a daring nudist-camp infiltration, to a romantic night on the town that gets someone killed. The cast is top-notch: Sanders and his brood make for effectively loathsome potential murderers and victims, Elke Sommer is charming and gorgeous, and Lom's outraged twitching is a work of art. But Sellers is the star attraction here, delivering pratfalls and double takes in a way that transcends ordinary slapstick. The members of Monty Python always knew the value of taking silliness seriously, and *Shot* is an example of the form at its height, before the Flying Circus ever opened its tent flaps.

What Monty Python did for comedy, the Beatles more than did for popular music. Both groups were wildly popular, hugely innovative, and helped define the course of their respective mediums for decades to come. But while Python never dabbled much in music, apart from the occasional comedy number, the Beatles made their comedy debut five years before *Flying Circus* hit the airwaves. It seems a bit unfair, really, that they'd make such a terrific show of it. Richard Lester's ***A Hard Day's Night*** (1964) is a low-key, laid-back fantasy for anyone who ever wondered what it would be like to spend a day tagging along with four lads from Liverpool who just happen to make up the most famous band in the world.

Turns out, it's about as fun as hanging out with your four best friends, although somewhat wittier and more prone to devolve into musical numbers. One of the more impressive aspects of *Night* is the way it manages to firmly set the public image of each band member, in a way that would stick with the group for the rest of their careers together. John is the cheeky one; Paul is the cute one; George is the quiet one; and Ringo is the mopey, slightly thick one. *Night* follows them over a typical day of work, as they try and escape from their legion of screaming fans, answer fan mail, deal with the press, and perform on live television. Paul's grandfather (well-known Irish television actor Wilfrid Brambell) tags along for the ride, trying to get over a broken heart and generally making a nuisance of himself.

Night is in some ways a cash-in, a promotional vehicle for an already wildly successful group whose name guaranteed that most every teenager in the English-speaking world would want a ticket. What's remarkable, then, is how well it holds up as a movie, even today. The clever dialogue, delivered as though it were no more than regular conversation, the cheery songs, the goofy energy, all add up to something that's joyous without ever becoming shrill or twee. The Pythons would be funnier than this, and edgier, but they would never be quite this delightful.

If *A Hard Day's Night* is an inadvertent classic, an attempt to exploit the Beatles' popularity on film that also just happens to be one of the greatest screen comedies of its era, then ***Help!*** (1965) is proof of just how lucky *Night*'s excellence really is. A continent-spanning chase film about a tribe of savages (led by Leo McKern) intent on sacrificing Ringo Starr to the god Kali, *Help!* is heavy-handed and overly twee where *Night* is deft and laid-back. Once more in the director's chair, Richard Lester sacrifices the low-key slyness of his previous collaboration with the Fab Four for over-the-top production design, winks to the audience, and frenetic slapstick. And, worst of all, the Beatles aren't quite up to the task of holding all the zaniness together, often appearing distracted or downright bored by the proceedings around them.

The story goes that parts of *Help!*'s script, with its lengthy interludes in the Alps and the Bahamas, were written to give the band a vacation to countries it had never visited before, and it shows. Hung on the thinnest of narratives—Ringo has a ring that McKern and his cronies want; chaos ensues—the movie has little in the way of narrative momentum, and much of its length feels haphazard and tossed off, for all its forced banter. So really, why watch it at all? The songs (which are, unsurprisingly, uniformly terrific) are available on the soundtrack, and most of the cast has done better work elsewhere.

The truth is, while *Help!* isn't perfect, it's still quite a lot of fun, to Beatles' fans, Pythonites, and anyone else who doesn't mind a bit of uncontrolled zaniness now and then. While McCartney, Starr, Lennon, and Harrison don't seem quite as present here as they did in *Night*, they're still generally charming and affably confused by the loonies that surround them. The film is gorgeous to look at, full of bright colors and beautiful vistas of foreign lands, and the different setting for each musical number makes them distinct and entertaining. There's something Pythonesque about the racially suspect foreigners intent on murdering a stranger for their bloodthirsty god, although with Monty Python, the joke would be as much about the inappropriate casting as it would be about the bloodlust. In its brazen, brassy, and sometimes blaring way, *Help!* is more of a precursor to *Flying Circus* than *Night* ever was.

There have been hundreds of portrayals of the Devil in film and television; it's an iconic, audience-friendly role that invites actors to put as distinctive a stamp as they can on the material. Peter Cook's Lucifer in ***Bedazzled*** (1967) may not be the greatest interpretation of the part ever put to screen, but if it isn't, it's pretty damn close. It's certainly the most affable, at any rate. In Cook's version, Beelzebub is a low-key charmer, a sly bastard who never lets on just how much he's kidding, the sort to lead souls to damnation via pranks and minor annoyances rather than overt acts of evil. This is a British Satan right down to his core: slightly mod, emptily polite, and capable of great and powerful magic, although he's not going to be showy about it or anything; that's simply not done.

Cook's Devil finds a somewhat willing dupe in Stanley Moon, a short-order cook with a problem. Moon (played by Cook's frequent partner Dudley Moore) has a terrible, passionate crush on Margaret (Eleanor Bron), a waitress who works with him, but because Stanley is such a shy, timid mouse of a man, he can't bring himself to ask her on a date. So he decides to commit suicide, but before he can succeed in his efforts, Lucifer arrives with a promising offer: if Stanley will simply sign over his soul, thus helping the Devil in his quest to have more souls at his disposal than God, Lucifer will grant him seven wishes with which to win his love. After some dithering, Stanley accepts the offer and starts wishing. But, seeing as how this is the Devil and all, those wishes have an unfortunate habit of not working out quite as he'd planned.

The plot is clever enough, creating something of a sketch-show feel for the film as Stanley jumps from each successive disappointing reality to the next, but the real pleasure of *Bedazzled* (and one that the 2000 remake, starring Brendan Fraser and Elizabeth Hurley, failed to capture) is the laid-back vibe that runs throughout—the sense that Cook and Moore's chats together are just a slightly skewed version of their usual conversations. Sight gags proliferate, and the bits and pieces we see of the edges of this Lucifer's domain (including a heavily advertised Raquel Welch as Lillian Lust) make for an inventive, inviting world. The narrative drive stays in the lower gears, but that works just fine; the movie has its share of belly laughs, but its greatest strength is its self-satisfied cleverness. That may sound like a criticism, but it isn't—the tone throughout matches Peter Cook's Devil to perfection: delightfully wicked, certainly up to no good, and entirely irresistible.

The Prisoner, Patrick MacGoohan's seminal science fiction series, isn't really a comedy. It has its funny scenes, and MacGoohan's mordant misanthropy hangs over every episode, but at heart, the show is a mind-bending thriller about the nature of identity and about the challenges facing a noncomformist in a society built on conformism. Which is just the sort of thing to appeal to the dedicated Python fan. The original *Flying Circus* was all about poking holes in cultural balloons full of hot air, and while it's doubtful *The Prisoner* (which ran from 1967 to 1968) influenced the Pythons directly, the show's artistic boldness and wit surely shares a common ground.

Patrick MacGoohan stars as Number Six, an ex-British agent who, upon quitting the service, is kidnapped and taken to the Village, a town for people who know too much to be allowed to run around free in the world. Over the course of seventeen episodes, Six struggles to escape from the Village and from whatever powers run the place—powers who, it becomes increasingly clear, are connected to the very highest levels of international government. Six fights against learning computers, mind-control, body-swapping, a murderous weather balloon named Rover, and, ultimately, himself. By the end, the series has gone from ambiguous adventure to mind-melting surrealism, with stops off in satire, time travel (hallucinatory), and spy games. It may not precisely make sense, but it never holds the viewer's hand or offers easy answers.

While the series doesn't operate on strict continuity (debates have raged over the proper episode-viewing order for decades), the short number of episodes means that anyone interested would be well advised to see the whole thing. Standouts include "Arrival," "Checkmate," "The Chimes of Big Ben," "A, B, C," "Many Happy Returns," and the two-part finale, "Absolute Zero" and "Free for All."

Comedy troupes don't always form overnight. The journey of how Monty Python became Monty Python has been told and retold in the years since the group achieved its peak success, but it's just as easy to watch the individuals find each other through the British shows that preceded the debut of *Flying Circus* in 1969. Like, for instance, **At Last the 1948 Show**. A sketch comedy series that debuted on ITV in 1967, *1948* has two Pythons, John Cleese and Graham Chapman, along with Tim Brooke-Taylor, Marty Feldman, and Aimi MacDonald. The resulting two-series show is a glimpse into where British sketch comedy stood in the years before Python came along and changed the rules forever.

Cleese and Chapman wrote together during *Flying Circus*, and at least one of the sketches here ("The Four Yorkshiremen," in which a group of upper-class gentlemen attempt to out-misery each other with tales of their childhoods) would eventually make its way to that series. But what's most interesting here is the blend of classic sketch presentation with the energy and encroaching madness that would come to define the Python years. The sketches run longer than Python sketches would, and many of them revolve around a slow build on a single concept, like Cleese's psychiatrist continually talking over Taylor's nervous patient, or Cleese and a guest actress struggling to stay in character during a live broadcast while tour guides explore the set behind them. These scenes wring every possible laugh out of an idea, but there's never connective tissue bridging them to other scenes in an episode. (This may at least partly be due to the fact that much of the show was destroyed.)

There's also a contrast between performance types. Taylor and Feldman mug for the audience—both actors do fine work, but they're clearly milking each line and strained facial expression for a response. Cleese and Chapman, on the other hand, work themselves into a frenzy, but neither actor appears to be much interested in whether or not the audience responds. It's a trait both would carry to their later work, that disinterest in pandering or playing for the crowd, and it would give *Flying Circus* a live-wire quality, a show that was so certain of its brilliance that it didn't need to slow down for the cheap seats. As it stands *At Last* is solid fun, a fine piece of history, and another piece of evidence of just how much Monty Python changed things.

A regular recurring theme of British comedy is the effect of annoying personalities on the typically reserved, decorous English psyche. Brits have a cultural obligation to face every difficulty with a stiff upper lip, miles of calm, and a patience so wooden you could build a bridge out of it. While this can be effective in most social situations, difficulty occurs when a true irritant arises: someone so pushy, so persistent, so aggravating that he can't be ignored, and yet simply punching him in the face would be considered bad form. A fair amount of Monty Python's humor came from such a conflict, and John Cleese's classic farce, *Fawlty Towers*, is practically the definitive statement on the topic. It's worth it, then, to see the seeds that would eventually bear such marvelous fruit: Cleese's 1968 television special ***How to Irritate People.***

The slightly-over-an-hour-long show is compromised largely of sketches demonstrating various principles of the process of irritation, with Cleese introducing each sketch with a brief monologue explaining the central idea. There are irritating parents, irritating restaurant hosts, irritating party guests, irritating boyfriends, irritating garage mechanics, irritating elderly women, and so on. The special is hit-or-miss, as many of the sketches (especially early in the show) take the main premise too literally, demonstrating actually annoying individuals and behavior without providing much in the way of laughs. It gets better as it goes, however, and *How to . . .* is still worth seeking out, for a number of reasons. There's Cleese himself, who occasionally looks a little stunned during his hosting duties (though this may be intentional), and the presence of Graham Chapman, Michael Palin, and Connie Booth makes this a sort of an embryonic Python presentation. Plus, some of the sketches work very well, especially a bit about airline pilots near the end, which has Cleese, Chapman, and Palin all working together.

John Cleese, Graham Chapman, Terry Jones, and Michael Palin in a scene from *Monty Python and the Holy Grail*. (Columbia Pictures/Photofest © Columbia Pictures)

2

THEN THERE WAS PYTHON

You could say that Monty Python did for comedy what the Beatles did for music. It'd be a painfully shallow overgeneralization, and anyone listening would almost certainly, and rightly, think you were a bit of a prat, but you could *say* it. Both groups took already established forms and changed them in ways that are still relevant today; both groups were hugely popular; both groups worked in roughly the same time period (the mid-to-late '60s, early '70s); and both groups were British. But the Beatles were all about precision, crafting perfect three-to-four-minute songs where each note, each word, was carefully considered. The band got looser as they went along, but that looseness was as much a sign of growing disillusionment with each other as it was artistic choice.

Compare that to Monty Python, which started in chaos and never really seemed to get out of it. The troupe of six members (Chapman, Cleese, Gilliam, Idle, Jones, Palin, with frequent support from Carol Cleveland and songwriter Neil Innes) started on the edge and stayed there for the duration. When ***Monty Python's Flying Circus*** (1969–1974) debuted, it seemed like the troupe could hardly get through a single episode without falling apart, let alone a series. From the very first sketch—"It's Wolfgang Amadeus Mozart"—a sense of anarchy pervades the air, as premise struggles against a constant influx of side gags and running jokes. Sketches don't end so much as stop, interrupted by other sketches, which are interrupted themselves by Terry Gilliam's bizarre animations. Characters address the camera and actors draw attention to their artificiality. It's a mess, but as it unfolds, it becomes more and more clearly a mess with a plan.

It's possible to view episodes of *Flying Circus* like symphonies, each one with its own distinct theme. That theme is introduced, then devolves into variations that weave in and out of each other until finally collapsing at the end into a grand mess of noise. Or maybe it's not like that at all. *Flying Circus* synthesized a number of influences—Spike Milligan, Peter Cook, and others—into something at once in keeping with what came before it, and at the same time completely new. The show feels fresh today, presaging modern comedy's digressive impulses and its running meta-commentary on its own silliness. Such an intensity of purpose couldn't sustain itself forever, though, and after its first two largely perfect series, *Flying Circus* started to show some cracks in the (still strong) third series. John Cleese left before the show's final six episodes.

Those cracks are evident in the troupe's big-screen debut, ***And Now for Something Completely Different*** (1971). Directed by Ian MacNaughton, who directed *Flying Circus*, the film was a collection of sketches from the television show's first two series, remade on film without the benefit of a studio audience. *Different*, with its greatest-hits format, was intended to introduce American audiences to the troupe, but the results were a pale version of Python at its finest. Running through old lines, the troupe does its best but seems a little tired, a little bored, and the film itself suffers as a result. Given the quality of the script, it's not a total wash, and completists will want to take a look, but by and large, Pythonites are better off sticking the TV show.

For their next film, ***Monty Python and the Holy Grail*** (1975), the group decided to put in more of an effort. *Holy Grail*, largely a spoof on the stories of King Arthur and the Knights of the Round Table, consisted of original material written expressly for the film, and the result is a movie far more engaging, both to the troupe and the audience, than *Different*. From the very start, *Grail* questions expectations, opening with a credits sequence over stark black that unravels into a treatise on the dangers of Sweden's moose population. From there, the story follows Graham Chapman as Arthur, the film's lone straight man, as he travels a mud-spattered, grim

English countryside, gathering fellow knights to obey God's will. (God Himself makes a cameo appearance.) Arthur's quest provides a spine to connect together a series of sketches on the horrible squalor of peasant life in the Middle Ages, the temptations that face the chaste knight, and the power of wizards.

Holy Grail is far more indicative of Python's knack for deconstruction than *Different*, and it's a much funnier movie as well, with bits (like the indomitable Black Knight, who persists in battle even after losing his limbs) that will be familiar touchstones for Pythonites. As a comedy, it's brilliant, but as movie with a beginning, middle, and end, it's uneven, the story routinely tossed aside in favor of digression. Python's next movie, **Life of Brian** (1979), would up the ante considerably for the group in terms of persistent storytelling, with a plot that remains relevant through the film's entire running time. Whether it or *Holy Grail* is superior is a question for the ages, but of all of Python's work, *Brian* is the only one that gives a damn if you like its leading man.

Chapman stars as Brian, a young man living in the Middle East in the time of Jesus Christ. The connection between the two is made with the movie's first scene, in which Brian's loud, sneering mother (Terry Jones) gets a visit from three Wise Men who don't realize that the stable they're actually looking for is a few buildings away. As a young man, Brian struggles to find his own identity in a city full of false prophets, lisping Romans, and squabbling revolutionaries. He tries to fight against the system, gets mistaken for a Messiah, and suffers horribly for it. *Brian* is as sketch-oriented as *Grail*, but the movie (which incited considerable controversy on release, although it avoids direct commentary on the Christian religion) has a clearer arc, with more of an investment in following its protagonist's adventures. As a result, it's the most consistent movie Python ever made, and possibly the best.

Monty Python often took its show on the road, for live concert productions of its best-known sketches and songs, and in 1982, before beginning production on what was to be the group's final movie, they released a movie of one of those concerts. **Monty Python Live at the Hollywood Bowl** is a lively snapshot of the team at the height of its popularity, playing to a crowd that hangs on their every word. By the time ***Monty Python's The Meaning of Life*** (1983) came out, that team was in its death throes. *Meaning of Life* was a retreat to the purely sketch-based format of *Different*, and while the material in *Life* is new, a definite sense of creative exhaustion pervades the entire film. Less a bad movie than a not-quite-great one, *Life* has its share of good bits, all loosely based around various stages of existence. Overall, though, the film's pervading sense of despair undercuts the comedy.

Outside the movies and television series, Monty Python did a number of record albums, which included sketches from the show, material from the movies, and material written expressly for the records themselves. ***The Instant Monty Python CD Collection***, a six-CD set from Virgin that collects a number of the albums together, is a good place to start for interested parties. There've been a number of Monty Python documentaries over the years detailing the troupe's history; the best of these is IFC's ***Monty Python: Almost the Truth*** (2009), a series of six hour-long episodes featuring interviews with surviving Pythons, as well as other prominent comedians and writers.

In the years following Python, each individual member would go his own way. There were occasional near reunions, like the series of charity concerts pulled together under the title ***The Secret Policeman's Balls*** (1976–1981). Held to benefit the human rights group Amnesty International, the four concerts feature Cleese, Palin, Jones, and (for the first concert) Chapman, reenacting some of their signature routines. The Balls also star other prominent contributors to English comedy like Peter Cook, Rowan Atkinson, Hugh Laurie, Dawn French, and other members of the original *Beyond the Fringe* revue. The resulting collaboration provides a rare opportunity to see British humor both old and new, as well as allowing the members of Monty Python to work with some of the performers who influenced them.

Flying Circus made its name partly because of its willingness to shrug off television convention—throughout its run, the series broke the fourth wall, interrupting its sketches with other sketches and generally thumbing its nose at anything resembling the old status quo. But when John Cleese chose to return to television in 1975, he would do so with a series that held strictly to one of the oldest forms of drama in existence: the classic farce. **Fawlty Towers** is as conventional as they come: each episode takes place almost entirely within one setting, scripts rigorously adhere to Chekov's rules, and characters do not change, mature, or learn moral lessons from their escapades. *Towers* is also perfect.

John Cleese stars as Basil Fawlty, a dreadful hotelier who loathes his guests, toadies to the upper class, and lives in terror of his wife, Sybill (Prunella Scales). To get through his day, he lords it over the help, including Manuel (Andrew Sachs), a waiter from Spain with a poor grasp of English, and Polly Sherman (Connie Booth, who was married to Cleese during the show's first series), a levelheaded student working at the hotel part-time to pay her way through school. The cast is perfect: Scales is a battle-axe, Sachs is a dervish, Booth is charming, and Cleese unleashes wave after wave of impotent fury. Each episode establishes a conflict relying on Basil's arrogance, obsession with social mores, and cowardice, and his every attempt to achieve his goals is thwarted by bad luck, selfish hotel guests, and his own essential stupidity.

It's difficult to precisely describe how effective this all is in practice. Cleese and Booth collaborated on each script, and their commitment to perfection shows through in the clockwork precision of the show. Farce depends on timing and rising comic momentum, and the structure of each episode of *Towers* is a master class in establishing various threats, and then resolving them together at the worst possible moment for all involved. There are no profound morals to be gleaned from events, and no arcs; the deepest the series gets is in the suggestion that prejudice and social climbing don't bring out the best in anyone. But even that's present entirely in the service of laughs. *Towers* received mixed reviews when its first series aired, but since then, it has come to be recognized as one of the greatest comedies ever made.

. . .

Flying Circus spent a considerable amount of time mocking the standard patterns of British television news documentaries, and Eric Idle brought that level of familiarity to this 1978 post-Python TV film, **The Rutles, or All You Need Is Cash.** Hosted by Idle himself as an unnamed news presenter, *Cash* charts the rise and fall of one of England's greatest fake bands. The Rutles, composed of Ron Nasty (Neil Innes, who wrote the groups' songs), Dirk McQuickly (Eric Idle), Stig O'Hara (Ricky Fataar), and Barry Wom (John Halsey), took the world by storm, then by cash, and finally by desperation, on a whirlwind career of greed, minor embarrassment, and tea-drinking. The Rutles made movies, changed the face of music in no way at all, and failed to catch the imagination of a generation.

What makes *Cash* so entertaining isn't simply that the Rutles' story is an obvious parody of the Beatles—it's the fact that the parody is so dead-on specific, riffing on trivia like the fact that Ringo Starr changed his name from Richard Starkey, or the "Paul is dead" myth, or the financial disaster of the Apple Boutique. Innes' music is dead on, close enough to the source material it parodies to be familiar without being a direct copy, and the run of celebrity cameos through the seventy-two-minute program (including Mick Jagger, Paul Simon, and, most impressively, George Harrison himself) lends the silliness an air of credibility that makes it even funnier. The Rutles began as a sketch, recorded a few albums, toured, and released a sequel to *Cash*, *The Rutles 2: Can't Buy Me Lunch*, in 2002, but the original show remains the group's peak, a snickering love letter to the greatest band of all time.

Terry Gilliam codirected *Monty Python and the Holy Grail* with Terry Jones. His first non-Python feature film, *Jabberwocky* (1977), isn't very good. Despite the presence of a game Michael Palin and the occasional funny bit, the story drags, with Gilliam's taste for grotesque realism undercutting most of the jokes. But **Time Bandits** (1981), his second solo project, demonstrated how his unique perspective could work on the screen. *Bandits* may run a bit longer than it needs to, but it's still a striking, imaginative, and frequently hilarious fantasy film, the work of a director finally realizing the tools he has at hand, and just how to use them.

A young boy named Kevin (Craig Warnock) hears things in his bedroom—strange things. His parents are so wrapped up in the television that they ignore his complaints, so one night he stays up—and sees a knight on horseback ride over his bed. Then a group of dwarfs fill the room. Led by Randall (David Rappaport), the dwarfs—the Time Bandits of the title, and former employees of the Supreme Being—have stolen a map of the holes in the space-time fabric of the universe. These holes allow them to travel to various points in time, and Randall and the others plan to use this power to steal history's greatest treasures. The plan isn't going well so far—and, unbeknownst to them, Evil (a terrific David Warner) is determined to get the map from them, and use it to rule the universe.

While *Bandits* isn't an official Python film, Michael Palin collaborated with Gilliam on the script, and Palin and John Cleese play characters. And *Bandits* is structured much like the best Python movies, as each separate historical era the Bandits (and Kevin) visit functions as a distinct sketch inside a larger story. But this is a Gilliam movie to the bone: full of mud, muck, charming monsters, and indifferent deities. The dialogue is quotable, the cast is top-notch, and the happy ending is surprisingly grim. With *Bandits*, Gilliam went from Python-at-large to a distinct artist.

Gilliam's fourth film, ***Brazil*** (1985), isn't exactly a comedy. It isn't exactly anything—a two-hour-plus mess of political satire, social commentary, black humor, and romance that defies convention at every turn. Jonathan Pryce stars as Sam Lowry, a low-level paper pusher living in a paper-pushing world. At night, Lowry dreams of a fantasy world where he's a winged warrior, slaying monsters and soaring through the air in pursuit of his ever-retreating ladylove. It's all a nifty symbol for the yearning of the common man to find transcendence in a tedious, humdrum universe, but Gilliam refuses to settle for easy answers. Lowry's underachieving lifestyle makes him a passive participant in a system that runs on bureaucratic brutality and indifference, but that changes when he finally meets the woman of his dreams. Jill Layton (Kim Greist) has a conscience, which means she tries to get involved when her downstairs neighbor is mistaken for a terrorist—which also means she is automatically marked as a terrorist herself for daring to question the system. Lowry takes it on himself to impress her, and in doing so finally wakes up to the nightmare he's spent his whole life ignoring.

There's a lot here to interest Python fans. Much as with *Time Bandits*, Gilliam brings a Python-esque sensibility to the film, mixing casual violence and absurdity with an aplomb familiar to anyone who's seen *Flying Circus* or *Holy Grail*. Michael Palin is the only group alum to show up on screen here, but it's one of his best roles in film, playing a disturbingly genial torturer whose bourgeois charms hide a chilling commitment to maintaining the party line. *Brazil* is chock-full of terrific ringers—Katherine Helmond is on hand as Lowry's looks-obsessed mother, Robert De Niro cameos as a revolutionary repairman, Ian Holm (another familiar face from *Bandits*) plays Lowry's dithering boss, and so on. *Brazil* loses *Bandits'* sketch-like approach to story, telling a bigger, more complicated plot that shows Gilliam's mad, sprawling genius to its best advantage. It's occasionally exhausting, but always astonishingly bold, and heartbreaking. It also serves as proof of the depth of the Python commitment to pointing out the absurdities of life: the more you mock, the less you laugh, and the harder it is to find your way back home.

Not to spoil anything, but neither *Time Bandits* nor *Brazil* has a traditionally happy ending. *Bandits* takes a child's point of view, and childhood always ends with the death of innocence, while *Brazil* is the adult look at life, which can't ever really escape the grim specter of death. It wasn't till his 1988 fantasy epic **The Adventures of Baron Munchausen** that Gilliam would finally see his way through to allowing his heroes to triumph, albeit in his own distinctively cynical fashion. *Munchausen* is life seen through the eyes of age and wisdom, and as such it acknowledges Death's existence while still refusing to accept the Grim Reaper's dominion. Where *Bandits* was shocked by mortality, and *Brazil* surrendered into madness, *Munchausen* posits that the only true way to live is to embrace the power of stories to transcend mortality. In a way, it shares its belief in the importance of fiction with *Brazil*, but where *Brazil*'s ending was tragedy, *Munchausen*'s is triumph.

John Neville stars in the title role as a brash, bold adventurer full of tales of brash, bold adventuring, many of which sound impossible, and all of which are probably lies. In an unidentified European city, the Baron regales a theater with his stories while war rages outside, until a child convinces him to dust off his adventuring shoes and save the day. What follows is balderdash coated with nonsense, served with a full helping of absurdity. *Adventures* has a semi-star-studded cast, including Robin Williams, Oliver Reed, and a young Uma Thurman, and former Python alum Eric Idle plays one of the Baron's trusted companions. It's an overstuffed movie that occasionally overstays its welcome, but has enough wonder and joy to make up for the slow spots.

The Fisher King (1991) is easily Terry Gilliam's most accessible film (with the possible exception of **Twelve Monkeys** [1995]). The script, by Richard LaGravenese, is a comparatively straightforward story of disgrace, wallowing, and redemption. It's a deeply romantic film, with little of the cynicism or misanthropy that colors the rest of Gilliam's work, and it's the definition of a "feel-good" picture. *King* was a moderate financial success as well as a critical one, and it helped earn Mercedes Ruehl an Academy Award for Best Supporting Actress. All of which is something of an odd fit for Gilliam's cinematic career. As a director, he's more used to working on the outside of the system, and *King* is crowd-friendly, not particularly challenging, and full of star Robin Williams doing the sort of Robin Williams shtick Robin Williams does best.

Thankfully, it's still a fine film. Jeff Bridges plays a shock jock who's built his career on poking people's buttons. He's at the peak of his career and ready to make the jump to his own television show when he makes the mistake of poking one particular button too hard: a lonely psychotic, after hearing Jeff's advice, snaps and goes on a killing spree at a fancy restaurant. Bridges' career implodes, and he winds up working at a video rental store, dating Mercedes Ruehl, and hiding from the world. One drunken night, he meets manic pixie dream homeless person Robin Williams. Williams isn't just any crazy hobo, though; he lost his wife in the massacre that ended Bridges' career. Now, in order to save his soul and get his life back on track, Bridges decides it his job to help Williams woo the girl of his dreams (Amanda Plummer) and get off the streets.

Plot-wise, there's not much more to it than that. Williams does his usual free-range ad-libbing, but the torment and sincerity behind the jokes helps them land, and Bridges, in a less showy but equally impressive turn, anchors the picture as a man who loathes himself so much he can barely stand to breathe. Ruehl and Plummer also do fine work, fleshing out love-interest roles with just enough raw-edged quirk. Also look for Michael Jeter as a homeless, cross-dressing cabaret singer with a penchant for songs from *Gypsy*. Terry Gilliam would do more subversive films, but rarely would he do one with this much heart.

It's not surprising that **A Fish Called Wanda** (1988) is hilarious. A caper comedy directed by Charles Crichton (who directed, among other films, *The Lavender Hill Mob*), written by John Cleese, and starring Cleese, Jamie Lee Curtis, Kevin Kline, and Michael Palin, isn't *guaranteed* to be funny, but as safe bets go, it's pretty damn close to a sure thing. No, what makes *Wanda* such an unexpected delight, to the point where it's still as lively and watchable today as it was when it was first released, is that there's a good-natured romance tucked neatly behind all the laughs. Romances in comedies tend to be largely one-note: a wacky man-child meets a responsible, attractive woman, and he must use his charms to woo her while simultaneously cleaning up his act just enough to imply he's reached the next stage of maturity. (For examples, please see the early films of Adam Sandler's career.)

Such is not the case with *Wanda*. The plot is clever enough: Curtis, Kline, and Palin are part of a group of thieves, led by Tom Georgeson (playing a character named George Thomason). After successfully managing to pull off a diamond heist, Kline and Curtis betray Georgeson to the police. There's a witness who saw him during the heist, and the case seems a lock, except Georgeson hid the loot before getting locked away, which means Curtis has to seduce the barrister, Cleese, handling the case. This upsets Kline, as he and Curtis are lovers, but he'd probably be even more upset if he knew Curtis was already planning on betraying him as soon as she got her hands on the stolen merchandise. And while all this is going on, Palin is trying his best to take out the witness, an old lady with a penchant for dog-walking.

All of this could've played well enough as a serious-minded noir, with Curtis as the perpetually twisty femme fatale, and a cast full of stooges falling in line to do her bidding. At the very least, one might expect more black comedy in a movie full of attempted murder and betrayal. Yet while *Wanda* isn't precisely toothless, it's a fundamentally sweet, charming film, where even the most loathsome character (Kline's Nietzsche-spouting buffoon) is really not all that loathsome. The relationship between Cleese and Curtis is the best indicator of this tonal shift. While most films would mock Cleese as a horny fool, *Wanda* allows him the dignity of a man who's spent his entire life in restrained despair, finally meeting someone who makes him happy to be alive. *Wanda* is well made, well acted (Kline won an Oscar for his performance, but really, everyone in the ensemble is equally good), and well worth checking out, both for the Python alum involved and for the terrific movie it is.

Of all the members of Monty Python, Graham Chapman is the only one who's been dead since 1989. In the last few years of his life, Chapman went on a series of comedy lecture tours in the U.S.; these tours were videotaped, and **Looks Like a Brown Trouser Job** (2005) is an edited-together collection of clips from his 1988 tour. Chapman looks gaunt on screen just months before he would pass away from cancer, but he's as lively and intelligent as ever, and there's no hint of maudlin self-pity or melancholy in his talks. Rather, the slightly-over-an-hour-long presentation is a reminder of what made Chapman such a key member of the troupe: a dry wit and cool exterior covering a mind capable of just about anything.

Over the course of *Trouser*, Chapman discusses his involvement with the Dangerous Sports Club (a group dedicated to the pursuit of, well, dangerous sports) and talks about his friendship with Keith Moon, drummer for the Who and general lunatic, before getting into his time with the Pythons and his experiences working on *Flying Circus* and the group's movies. It's a talk that starts slow but gains speed as it goes, with Chapman's level tone and openness making for a likable, engaging performance. *Trouser* doesn't purport to be a history of Python, or even an autobiography of its star, but it does provide an entertaining, and occasionally revealing, glimpse into one of the men responsible for a hilarious revolution.

Dan Aykroyd and John Belushi take on Richard Nixon and Henry Kissinger on *Saturday Night Live*. (NBC/Photofest © NBC)

3

SKETCH COMEDY AFTER PYTHON

While Monty Python may have perfected the art of sketch comedy, after they left the scene, their absence created a void that talented writers and performers have been working to fill ever since. Please enjoy this list of the ones who came after Python and made the format of sketch their own.

In 1997, Michael Palin and John Cleese performed the Dead Parrot sketch on an episode of *Saturday Night Live* (1975–), the long-running American live sketch comedy television show. The Dead Parrot sketch is one of Monty Python's best-known, best-loved bits, centered on a man with a deceased pet bird, and the shop clerk who refuses to acknowledge the corpsified state of said bird. It plays off the absurdity of the clerk's increasingly strained responses, and the customer's rising irritation at the clerk's implacability. The sketch first aired in 1969, in episode 8 of *Flying Circus*'s first season, and was very, very funny. Only, when Palin and Cleese performed the bit almost thirty years later, the audience wasn't responding to the sketch as written so much as it was responding to the sketch's iconic status. Cleese and Palin's performances were disinterested, going-through-the-motions, and the applause and laughter they got had been earned before they even stepped on stage. Really, it's that kind of automatic approval that's sustained *SNL* for over three decades on the air. It's a show that started great, hit some rough patches, and has settled into a low-level mediocrity that keeps going largely on the goodwill of what it once was.

Thankfully, what it once was, was something pretty great. When *SNL* debuted, watching new episodes felt like getting a peek into the hippest party in town. Episode length would vary over time, but the basic model that would sustain the entire series was evident from the start: each episode was hosted by a comedian, actor, or popular entertainer (four members of Python have appeared on the show; Eric Idle and Michael Palin have both hosted). The host would get a monologue at the start, and then a series of unconnected sketches, split between live bits and ad parodies, made up the bulk of the episode, along with a performance (or two) by a musical act. From the start, live sketches leaned on the strength of the cast to carry them, but the original cast still stands as one of the greatest collections of comedy talent ever brought together in a single ensemble: Chevy Chase, John Belushi, Dan Aykroyd, Jane Curtin, Gilda Radner, and Garrett Morris. The show would serve as a launching point for many of its performers to film careers, and Chase left after the first season to be replaced by Bill Murray. The cast stayed largely consistent for the next three years, establishing a legend that remains the show's most enduring legacy.

Watching the early episodes of *SNL* now, what's most impressive is how loose and experimental the series was at the start. The first season had Muppets, which didn't work, and short films by Albert Brooks, which did. The skits weren't always strong (given the demands put on the show's writers to provide new material every week while the season is airing, episodes tend to have a few strong concept sketches, and bits that rely on obvious sight gags and performers to fill in the empty spaces), but they were made up for by the ensemble's energy, and the shaky, exciting feeling that important things were happening, even if those important things sometimes involved John Belushi dressed as a giant bee. *SNL* is an easy show to make fun of these days, and to bemoan how far it's fallen from what it once was, but the truth is, the series' biggest strength and weakness was always its willingness to try anything, and most of it more than once.

. . .

Somewhere in America, there's a small town known as Melonville. And, unlike many small towns, Melonville has its own special television station. Under the guidance of Guy Caballero (Joe Flaherty), the greedy station owner so desperate for respect that he spends most of his time on-screen riding in a wheelchair he doesn't in fact need, *Second City Television (SCTV)* (1976–1984) brings adventure, music, comedy, and romance to the screen on a very tight budget. Station manager Edith Prickley (Andrea Martin) uses her job to pick up dates; director and egotistical star Johnny La Rue (John Candy) scrambles for cash; and shmoozy talk-show host Sammy Maudlin (Flaherty) holds court for singer sex-kitten Lola Heatherton (Catherine O'Hara) and professional suck-up Bobby Bitman (Eugene Levy). It's all hilarious, although probably not in a way any of them recognize.

Second City has a long and fairly convoluted history on TV. These days, it's best remembered from its fourth and fifth seasons, which aired on NBC from 1981 to 1983. Tracing its origins back to Toronto's Second City stage show, the series used the model of a low-rent TV station to tie together a wide variety of sketches and satirical bits, from movie parodies (like a terrific Woody Allen / Bob Hope mash-up with Rick Moranis and Dave Thomas called *Play It Again, Bob*), to bad cable ads, to awkward *American Bandstand* rip-offs, to anything else that plays in the wee hours of the morning on the low end of the dial. In between programs, Caballero tries his best to sell out, and various other personalities mingle and spar in an ongoing struggle for money and screen time.

The result is one of the greatest sketch comedy shows ever produced, a hugely influential series that manages coherent storylines, oddly moving character moments, and genial slapstick with equal ease. *SCTV* was a training ground for performers who would go on to big-screen careers. Unlike Monty Python, its sketches tended to run long, and the show was not afraid to be topical, or to rely on the ability of its actors to impersonate real-life stars and musicians. Rick Moranis in particular was the king of this—his Woody Allen is barely distinguishable from the real thing—but the show also made use of its cast's knack for impressions of pop culture archetypes that suggested familiarity without being tied down to any specific name. The result is a brutal satire of insecurity and showbiz phoniness that never comes across as mean-spirited or dated, and the show still holds up well today, even after many of its touchstones have faded into obscurity.

Sketch comedy is ephemeral stuff. In roughly five to seven minutes, characters must be drawn sharply enough to register, a concept must be explained, and that concept must be exploited to the fullest possible extent. The form can vary, but generally speaking, sketch comedy doesn't much go in for depth. This can be exhausting in the long term, and given that sketches are even more hit-or-miss than other forms of comedy (since they can't rely on emotional investment or plot momentum to cover a bad joke), it's no surprise that the format is largely relegated to television and the stage. Full-length feature films made entirely of comic skits rarely work. Even Monty Python struggled with the form—*And Now for Something Completely Different* fumbled in part because it was simply a collection of the best bits of *Flying Circus*, without any connective tissue holding them together.

Still, the passionate Pythonite will recognize that part of the pleasure of being a student of comedy is enduring the mediocre for the occasional shining moment of greatness. To that end, two feature-length American sketch comedy films present themselves: **The Kentucky Fried Movie** (1977) and **Amazon Women on the Moon** (1987). Despite being released a decade apart, the two movies have a surprising amount in common. Both mix sketches with long-form genre parody; both feature work by director John Landis; and both feature a surprising number of topless women, always a fallback for comedy that isn't sure it can deliver on laughs. Both films are a long way from perfect, but there's enough here that works to make them of interest to Pythonites.

Kentucky Fried Movie is best known these days as being the film debut of David Zucker, Jim Abrahams, and Jerry Zucker, the team that would eventually bring the world *Airplane!* and *The Naked Gun*, among others. On *KFM*, the trio sticks to writing, with Landis taking credit as the film's sole director. Outside of a handful of cameos from stars like Donald Sutherland and Billy Bixby, the cast is made up of unknowns who remained unknown even after the picture was released. Sketches include parodies of the nightly news, exploitation films, and infomercials, with the centerpiece being an extended *Enter the Dragon* riff called *A Fistful of Yen*.

While *KFM* is mostly famous for bringing its writing team into the mainstream, *Amazon Women on the Moon* boasts a cast of up-and-comers (like Arsenio Hall, Phil Hartman, and Michelle Pfeiffer, among others), and a whole team of directors, two of whom (Landis and Joe Dante) were already well known for popular genre films. *AWotM* has slightly more of a plot than *KFM*, nominally being made up of the late-night ads, programs, and movies being aired on the struggling channel 8 WIDB-TV. There are more commercial parodies here, as well as sketches that mock celebrity roasts, film critics, and *The Invisible Man*. The titular movie-in-a-movie is a parody of fifties sci-fi schlock, most specifically *Queen of Outer Space*. The parody jokes about *Queen*'s over-the-top sexism and cheap sets, the real joke being that it can't quite top the real thing.

KFM and *AWotM* show the strengths and weaknesses of the format they work in. Both movies live and die on the strength of the material, and not all the material is strong enough to sustain the attention; and both movies jump from idea to idea fast enough to avoid getting too bogged down in any one bad gag. Pythonites will enjoy the highlights and appreciate the way the weaker spots demonstrate just how remarkable the consistency of Monty Python really was.

A Bit of Fry & Laurie (1987–1995) is not always precisely funny. Like all sketch comedies, some jokes don't land, but it's more than that. Stephen Fry and Hugh Laurie are undeniably clever and hilarious, and there are laughs to be found in all four of the show's series. But most sketch shows operate on one basic principle: taking a premise (like "The parrot is dead, but the pet-store owner will not acknowledge this," or "Someone writes a joke so funny that it can be used for the war effort"), and wringing as many gags as possible out of that premise for however long that sketch lasts. To do this, the sketch will start by establishing the premise and playing that premise out directly, and then tries various permutations of the original idea, until, at best, it builds to a surprising, hilarious conclusion.

When this works, it's brilliant, but when timing is off, or the premise weak, it can be exhausting, like listening to a stranger waste five minutes to tell the world's worst joke. *Fry & Laurie* follows the basic sketch structure plenty of times, but it's also more than happy to take the laid-back approach. Fry and Laurie clearly take great delight in language just for the sake of language, and much of their humor comes from the absurd ways people can use modes of speech to elevate themselves or distract from their situation. Plenty of bits on the show revolve around Fry ejaculating elaborate verbal pyrotechnics while Laurie plays an increasingly baffled straight man, and there's little in the way of variation or build. Which means, again, it's not always funny. But it's so genial and entertaining that it doesn't have to be funny. At its best, the show is witty and gut-busting. At worst, it's witty and endearing. The fourth (and last) series is the weakest, but all are worth the time of the Pythonite.

And anyone who's seen all four series and still isn't full up on the undeniable chemistry of the two leads would be well advised to check out ***Jeeves and Wooster*** (1990–1993). An adaptation of the "Jeeves" stories by P. G. Wodehouse, the show cast Laurie as the bumbling goofball Bertie Wooster, a genially immature young man of wealth and few responsibilities; Fry costars as Bertie's indefatigable valet, Jeeves, whose remarkable ability to protect his master's interests and handle even the most delicate calamity comes in very handy. Each episode of the show follows a similar structure: some seemingly intractable problem threatens to upend Wooster's blissful existence. Bertie will attempt to solve the problem and fail miserably, almost certainly making the situation worse, and then Jeeves will step in and make everything okay with a few deft moves. It's a structure that can get old fast, but Laurie and Fry fill both their roles admirably well, and at times the show plays almost like the longest-running *Bit of Fry & Laurie* sketch ever filmed; there's something charming in its resolute predictability.

. . .

Maybe the easiest way to explain how **The Kids in the Hall** (1988–1994) worked at its best is to show the troupe (which shares the same name as its five-season television series) at its worst, in their 1996 film feature debut, **Brain Candy**. *Candy* is the story of a hapless scientist (Kevin McDonald) who stumbles across the secret to perpetual happiness in pill form. His discovery is immediately seized upon and exploited by a ruthless drug company, rocketing the scientist to soul-destroying fame and fortune. Unfortunately, in the rush to get the happy pills on the street, the medication wasn't properly tested, and soon users find themselves locked in perpetual bliss, experiencing their most perfect memory over and over and over again. And thus, society crumbles.

Candy isn't a terrible movie, and, if they approach it with the proper expectations, curious Pythonites will find a fair amount to enjoy in its running time. But there's no denying that the movie fails to live up to the brilliant legacy the Kids built for themselves on TV. A certain creative exhaustion pervades the film, as the group was squabbling amongst themselves during filming even more so than usual, and that exhaustion leads to weak jokes and, even worse, a constant feeling of contempt for the characters and their misadventures. The writing on *The Kids in the Hall* is more consistently strong than in the film, and, just as importantly, the troupe has an obvious fondness for all the weird, irritating, pathetic, needy characters they create. Comedy can be effectively cruel, but there's something to be said for goodwill through mockery, and the Kids have it in spades.

Maybe it's a Canadian thing. The troupe, made up of McDonald, Scott Thompson, Mark McKinney, Bruce McCulloch, and Dave Foley, formed in Toronto in 1985. After a brief breakup when McKinney and McCulloch went to work on *Saturday Night Live*, the group reformed in 1986, eventually to be discovered by *SNL* producer Lorne Michaels, and their own television series debuted on Canadian television in 1988. Each half-hour episode of the series is a collection of sketches and monologues performed by members of the group; the sketches vary from simple character skits (like an argument between Foley and McDonald about the name of a movie about an old man who misses his sled) to far more ambitious filmed bits that pushed the expectations of what sketch work could be, albeit in a polite, ingratiating manner. The show was also noteworthy for dealing with gay themes; the openly gay Thompson managed to mock and celebrate homosexual stereotypes, most notably as the effeminate party enthusiast Buddy Cole.

Through all of it, a general spirit of cheery foolishness pervades. Monty Python viewed the characters in the majority of its work as tools to get ideas and gags across, but the Kids have a definite fondness for even the most foolish of their targets. Along with the strong performers and writing, that fondness is one of the reasons the show lasted as long and aged as well as it did. After separating to work on various projects after the failure of *Brain Candy*, and doing the occasional tour together, the Kids reunited on the screen in 2010 for the generally well-received eight-episode miniseries **Death Comes to Town.**

Great sketch shows often have a strong sense of place. *Flying Circus*'s version of London, all vicious nun gangs and Piranha brothers, defined the city to outsiders for years; *SNL* makes a point of pride out of its New York home; and *Kids in the Hall* was very, very Canadian. (Yes, all of it.) In this spirit, there's **The Ben Stiller Show** (1992–1993). The short-lived series started in a short run on MTV from 1990 to 1991, but the version that's available today on DVD came to Fox in 1992, only to be canceled after twelve episodes because of low ratings. The thirteen episodes that exist today show young stars before they'd come into their own, an impressively consistent comic vision, and some terrific writing by artists who would go on to dominate the industry. And the show is about as profoundly Hollywood, California as it's possible for a television show to be.

Partly this is due to the episode format. Each week, Stiller introduces himself to the camera and takes the audience on a tour through sunny streets, backlot sets, and the hills overlooking the city, chatting with a guest star and members of the cast before introducing new sketches. And part of the Hollywood feel comes from the material of the sketches themselves. Stiller is a talented impressionist, and the show makes frequent use of his abilities, taking on celebrities like Tom Cruise, William Shatner, Bruce Springsteen, and Jay Leno. Sketches often revolved around mixing and matching popular movies and TV shows, like "Cape Munster," which puts Eddie Munster into the Robert De Niro role in a parody of Martin Scorsese's *Cape Fear.* The show also lampooned show-business standbys like the sleazy, anything-for-a-buck agent, and featured cameos from comedians like Roseanne and Garry Shandling.

With only thirteen episodes, *The Ben Stiller Show* never really got a chance to get old, but it never entirely settled into its own voice, either. Still, the comedy remains as smart and biting as it ever was, even if the hipness has faded a little over the years. The talent pool is impressive; the show's four main cast members, Stiller, Janeane Garofalo, Andy Dick, and a pre–*Mr. Show* Bob Odenkirk, would go on to bigger fame in other projects, and the writing staff includes Judd Apatow and a pre–*Mr. Show* David Cross, among others. *The Ben Stiller Show* may not have the body of work of other sketch shows, but it's a great look back at the state of comedy in the early '90s, especially if you want to get some of that warm California air circulating in your living room.

One of the secrets to cult success is limited access. To build the devotion of a small group of followers to pitch-perfect intensity, the object of their fandom needs to be something that's more talked about than seen. ***The State*** (1993–1995) originally aired a three-season run on MTV, a total of twenty-six episodes, before the group that created it (also called "The State") decided to move on to another network. This went badly, and the show left television after a final, poorly advertised and low-rated special on CBS. In the years since, fans who caught those original twenty-six episodes have been clamoring for a DVD release. By the time an official set hit shelves in 2009, the show's legend was so pronounced, it almost didn't matter if it was good or not; fans were so committed, they were already seeing greatness.

Thankfully, *The State* is pretty great—maybe not the absolute pinnacle of sketch comedy television, but funny, creative, and deserving of its politely rabid fan base. Founded by Todd Holoubek in the late '80s, the State (originally called "The New Group") was a group of eleven twenty-something aspiring comedians and improv vets. After building a reputation in New York, the group worked on MTV's *You Wrote It, You Watch It* show with host Jon Stewart before clinching a deal for their own series. The resulting show (which the group wrote, directed, performed, and edited themselves) followed in the vein of *The Kids in the Hall*, with its tangentially related individual skits punctuated by occasional direct appeals to the audience by the cast as "themselves."

State had good writing and a bigger-than-usual cast, many of whom would keep working together after the series ended, on shows like *Reno 911!* (2003–2009), *Children's Hospital* (2010–) , and *Party Down*. The sketches tend towards the silly side of the line, and while the troupe has one female performer, Kerri Kenney, a number of the male comics maintain the longstanding tradition of the form by working in drag in those instances where a man in a dress would be funnier than a girl in one. Memorable bits include a couple who have found an unusual use for Muppets; Doug (Michael Showalter), an adolescent eager to fight back against a largely compliant world; and Louie (Ken Marino), whose primary character trait is his nonsensical catchphrase, "I wanna dip my balls in it." *The State* isn't particularly cutting-edge, although it did take some creative risks by the end of its run in much the same way the Kids experimented with film styles. Mostly, though, it's just a lighthearted goof that ended before it had a chance to get old.

Not all comedy comes from rage, but plenty of it does. Angry sketches don't always work; humor can be an effective weapon, but the more focused it is on a specific target, the greater the danger that the righteousness will drown out the comedy. There's no question that Bob Odenkirk and David Cross, the creators of ***Mr. Show*** (1995–1998), are pissed off. They're annoyed by hypocrites, commercialization, greed, shallow exploitation, stupidity, and pretty much everything that makes America awful. But while their frustration may have inspired some of their writing, the jokes come first: *Mr. Show* is edgy, biting, and cutting-edge. Most importantly, it's funny as hell.

Over the course of four seasons and two specials, Odenkirk and Cross worked together to poke holes in the fevered egos of the monied and powerful. Each episode started with the two performers on stage before a live audience; they'd introduce the week's major theme or premise, and the sketches themselves would flow from one to the next through a sort of dream logic. The show was willing to be topical, as with its vicious takedown of Eric Clapton's Grammy-winning "Tears in Heaven," featuring Cross as a maudlin musician with a habit of exploiting personal tragedy (including his own death) for award gain. But some sketches are built on pure premise, like Cross's turn as a pre-taped call-in TV show.

In addition to Bob and David, *Mr. Show* boasts an impressive cast, including future animation stars Tom Kenny and Jill Talley, and up-and-coming comics like Sarah Silverman, Brian Posehn, Jack Black, Paul F. Tompkins, and Patton Oswalt. Odenkirk and Cross would try and bring the series to the big screen with a feature-length version of one of their most popular sketches, *Run, Ronnie, Run* (2002), with mixed-to-poor results. (Although it's worth checking out for Mandy Patinkin's cameo alone.) But the original show holds up well. While many of the series' best gags come out of anger, *Mr. Show* never comes across as strident. It's childish in the best way, profane, unsparing, often dark, but never grim.

On March 12, 1996, families who had just gotten laughing at the nonthreatening antics of Tim Allen on ABC's *Home Improvement* settled in for the debut of ***The Dana Carvey Show***. Carvey, whose film career had stalled after a series of low-performing duds, was best known for his seminal work on *Saturday Night Live*, notably his impersonations of public figures like Ross Perot, and original characters like the Church Lady and Garth, Mike Myers's partner in the wildly successful *Wayne's World* franchise. His comedy was irreverent, occasionally childish, and often pointed, but it was rarely shocking, which meant audiences were unprepared for the *Carvey Show*'s first sketch.

Carvey, done up as then President Bill Clinton, addresses the nation, gloating over his strong poll numbers and promising to cut his wife, Hillary Clinton, out of the Oval Office. Carvey-as-Clinton explains that he wants to provide sustenance to the world, and to that end, he's gone an intense round of hormonal therapy and now has teats for the suckling. He proceeds to demonstrate the efficacy of those teats, giving suck first to a baby doll, then to puppies and cats. Words can't capture the off-putting nature of the sketch; it's more shocking than funny, and sets a tone for the rest of the show that had viewers changing the channel in droves. Advertisers dropped the series, and ABC canceled it after seven episodes.

Which is a shame, because past that opening sketch (which isn't awful, really), *The Dana Carvey Show* is a strong, innovative comedy show, employing a host of rising talent and a sharp take on politics and pop culture, as well as a willingness to mock its own conventions. With a creative team including Charlie Kaufman (*Being John Malkovich*), Louis C.K. (*Louie*), Stephen Colbert (*The Colbert Report*), and Steve Carrell (*The 40-Year-Old Virgin*), the show is now seen as ahead of its time, and a proving ground for writers and performers who would come to define the industry. Classic sketches include "Skinheads from Maine," a news program that hides upsetting information behind extreme cuteness, and the show's routine skewering of its commercial sponsors. The entire eight-episode series is available on DVD.

Big Train's (1998–2002) most famous alum to American audiences is probably Simon Pegg, of *Hot Fuzz* and *Star Trek* fame. On *Train*, Pegg is a member of a strong ensemble that includes Kevin Eldon, Mark Heap, Julia Davis, and Catherine Tate, among others. The show uses its cast well, switching between one-on-one dialogue sketches and larger ensemble pieces. *Train* ran for two series of six episodes apiece, the first in 1998 and the second in 2002; it was created by Arthur Mathews and Graham Linehan, who were also responsible for *Father Ted*.

The majority of *Big Train*'s sketches are based off an engine that has generated much of Britain's best comedy: the English commitment to decorum and etiquette, contrasted against a series of surreal, and occasionally horrifying, invasions into normal life. Like, for example, a company Jesus who has to fire a disruptive employee who just happens to be the Devil, or an office work force that objects when their boss threatens to take away their "wanking" privileges. *Train* isn't quite as solid as the best of sketch comedy, as it often relies too much on the initial cleverness of a premise, milking an idea without escalating it beyond the initial shock of recognition. Which means the show doesn't offer many surprises beyond its sketches' hooks, but thankfully, those hooks are generally strong. The performances are solid, and the writing is consistent. And it's a great chance to catch a glimpse of the men and women who went on to be the defining faces of British comedy.

Along those lines, there's also **Not the Nine O'Clock News** (1979–1982), which ran for twenty-seven episodes. Presented as a jokey alternative to the BBC's less sketch-based nine o'clock news program, *Not . . .* starred Rowan Atkinson, the man who would be Blackadder, as well as Pamela Stephenson, Mel Smith, and Griff Rhys Jones. The show used editing and special effects to string together short and long sketches about music acts, politics, game shows, and other deeply ridiculous things. The writers often lampooned real news stories of the time, which may cut down on the show's re-watchability, but some bits, like Atkinson's memorable take on Barry Manilow, will hopefully live forever. The show helped launch Atkinson's career and helped mark the tone of the modern sketch show: irreverent, sophisticated, broad, and not all that different from the Flying Circus that inspired it.

In general, Monty Python shied away from making grand social statements or overly specific satire. While the troupe did its fair share of parody, there was never any sense from *Flying Circus* or any of the movies that Python was trying to change the world or teach anyone a moral lesson (apart from *Life of Brian*'s basic "Hey, maybe we should stop being assholes, although that probably won't keep us from being crucified in the end"). You could say, at its deepest, the group's core goal was to add to the supply of silliness in the world. The ***Upright Citizens Brigade*** (1998–2000), a sketch show that aired for three seasons and thirty episodes, continues this aim in style. At the start of each episode, a serious narrator explains the group's primary goal: to sow chaos through society. There are worse goals to have.

The *Brigade* started life as an improvisational troupe in Chicago. The television series featured the group's most recent and best-known roster: Matt Besser, Amy Poehler, Ian Roberts, and Matt Walsh. Each episode introduces the members of the brigade, re-states their mission, and then follows a series of loosely connected sketches, all generally built around a distinct theme. Besser, Poehler, Roberts, and Walsh play all major roles themselves, in addition to their ongoing distinct UCB personae. The segments set inside the UCB's mission control (which is located deep under the earth, ob-viously) give the show an added cohesion, and while none of the UCB personae are particularly deep, their personalities are distinct and stay basically consistent, helping to distinguish the show from other sketch series.

Since the UCB started as a live show, the TV series works in a fair amount of material in front of audiences not entirely prepared for what they're about to see. The performers here are all strong, with Poehler being a particular standout; it's no surprise she's the breakout star of the group, going on to *Saturday Night Live*, movies, and her current series, *Parks and Recreation*. The idea that all the sketches on *Brigade* had a purpose behind them means that each individual bit doesn't necessarily live and die on its own. Instead, every subversive, snickering moment is part of a grand scheme of anarchy. The men who created the People's Front of Judea (née the Judean People's Front) would surely approve.

The UCB is as much an improv group as a scripted one, and since their original series was canceled the group has continued to perform on stage together and with special comedy guest stars. This live show, ***ASSSSCAT***, is available on DVD. Given the nature of the medium, it's not as tightly constructed as the group's televi-sion series. Even in the hands of gifted performers, improvisation is largely about the energy between the performers and the live audience, which doesn't always translate to video. But *ASSSSCAT* is successful, and a great glimpse of talented performers going back to where they began.

Python never did much with scary material, but they understood the value of horror in comedy. Take, for instance, the sketch "The Funniest Joke in the World," first performed in the first episode of the first series of *Flying Circus*, and later recreated (though in shorter form) for the troupe's first movie, *And Now for Something Completely Different*. The premise is one of Python's best: a poor writer ("Ernest Scribbler," heh) one day writes the funniest joke in the world. The joke is so funny, in fact, that just reading it back to himself causes him to die from laughter. His wife comes up to his study, finds his body, reads the joke herself, and dies as well. Then the police show up and one by one succumb to the joke's deadly humor content. The army, realizing they have a potent weapon against the Nazis, has the joke translated into German (one word at a time, to save lives), and throws it into the hands of soldiers in the Second World War.

It's a hilarious sketch, one that starts with a great concept and then develops that concept in logical, surprising ways. And there doesn't seem to be anything malevolent about it. But when you break it down—well, the idea here is that someone finds a combination of words so powerful that it causes instant death. There's no protection against it and no easy way to grasp what's happening; the moment anyone tries to deconstruct the joke itself, he's a goner. It'd be a decent enough setup for a horror movie, if it were presented as anything slightly less than ridiculous; and in that context, it's not hard to imagine just such a joke coming from the town of Royston Vasey, the home of ***The League of Gentlemen*** (1999–2002). A British series about the horrible things folks in small towns can get up to in their spare time, *League* strikes a balance between dark comedy and outright scares and, when in doubt, leans towards the latter. Here there are certainly jokes that can kill, but it's uncertain if you'll leave this world laughing when they strike.

The League is made up of four men: Jeremy Dyson, Mark Galiss, Steve Pemberton, and Reece Shearsmith. This quartet writes the series (which started as a radio show and eventually wound up on the big screen with 2005's *The League of Gentlemen's Apocalypse*) and plays the majority of Royston's twisted, off-putting residents. There's the couple that runs the Local Shop, committed to protecting the town against outside influence; the woman who runs classes for the unemployed, who hates the unemployed with a passion; the cab driver getting ready for his sexual reassignment surgery; and the butcher who has a special meat that comes from—well, best not to ask too many questions. The show's first series is its closest to traditional sketch comedy, following various threads through six episodes while also taking time for one-offs and shorter bits. The show isn't for everyone, but its unsparing tone, something like a mix of Edward Gorey and John Waters, is hypnotic for those who see the appeal and are, of course, local.

In *Looks Like a Brown Trouser Job*, Graham Chapman describes the struggles he and John Cleese had in bringing one of their sketches to the screen. The bit centered on a man going to a funeral parlor looking for help in handling the body of his late mother. The funeral parlor offers a variety of increasingly tacky solutions, treating the corpse like a bit of rubbish or potential firewood, before settling on the possibility of cooking Mom up for a bit of a snack. At first, the son is shocked, but he then admits to being peckish. The sketch was deemed so offensive that the only way Cleese and Chapman were able to get it on air was to have the in-studio audience vocally express their disgust throughout the filming, before finally rising up in fury and chasing the two performers off the stage. So Monty Python had its share of controversy; but never in the entire run of *Flying Circus* did they take the sort of risks Dave Chappelle and Neal Brennan took on their series **Chappelle's Show** (2003–2006).

It's not that Python shied away from risky material; more that *Chappelle's Show*, which ran for two full seasons on Comedy Central before Chappelle's abrupt departure led to a severely truncated third season, was more looking to get laughs by questioning social prejudice than Python ever was. *Chappelle's Show* was often, and often aggressively, about race, about the stereotypes people have and pretend they don't, about the persistent absurdity of double standards, bigotry, and how some people prefer large butts to smaller butts. The show format has Chappelle coming out on stage at the start of each episode to run the audience through a series of previously taped sketches and occasional musical interludes. This creates a loose, personal feel to the series, almost as though each segment were really just part of Chappelle's stand-up brought to life.

One of *Chappelle's Show*'s most indicative sketches was also one of its first, a *Frontline* parody that aired in the show's first episode. The sketch, which centers on a blind African American who, not realizing he's black, has risen to prominence in the Ku Klux Klan for his fervent hatred of blacks and all other non-white races, is a sharp satire of the idiocy of hate groups, and drew attention for its frequent (and necessary) use of the word "nigger." But behind all the satire and word choice, what really stand out are the clever concept and the smart build to the final gag. *Chappelle's Show* was more direct about race than sketch comedy (or any comedy) traditionally gets, but it also earns every provoking gag (and not every sketch is confrontational) through fearless, solid writing. The series wasn't perfect, and some bits have aged better than others, but it remains a striking example of the power of comedy to confront the taboo, without softening its edge or forgetting the punch lines.

Nobody ever said sketch comedy was easy; while sitcoms can mine familiar character relationships for storylines and laughs, relying on audiences' emotional investment in a recurring ensemble to pull through any rough patches, sketch comedies don't have this luxury. Every segment lives or dies on its concept and writing, and while a great performance can save a mediocre premise, that only goes so far. Even great comedy writers can run dry on ideas over the course of a twenty-plus-episode season, which may be one of the reasons ***That Mitchell and Webb Look*** (2006–) is such a strong show; following the British model, at four series of six episodes apiece, it's never had to risk wearing out its welcome. Of course, the duo started on the radio with ***That Mitchell and Webb Sound***

(2003–2009), and they've also got a book out, and David Mitchell does these terrific video podcasts ... So maybe the reason *Mitchell and Webb* is so great has nothing to do with fewer episodes, and everything to do with writers and performers who really, really know their stuff.

Look has a firm foundation of recurring sketches: there's "Numberwang," the inexplicable game show of numbers and wanging; "Get Me Hennimore!," a satire of stale '70s TV farce; a guy who charges fees for deadly tourist attractions; "The Surprising Adventures of Sir Digby Chicken Caesar," about a drunk who fancies himself a master detective; and others. What makes these recurring bits work is what makes the show on the whole so successful: even sketches with regular structures find new ways to explore their premise, expanding on old ideas without failing to hit what made them effective in the first place.

This translates to classic sketch comedy done with considerable aplomb and wit. *Look* isn't as subversive as Python at its height; meta-humor and deconstruction have been an accepted element in the format for decades, and the show simply delivers the ideal version of familiar forms. The stars, David Mitchell and Morgan Webb, took what they learned from previous collaborations (*Peep Show*, the aforementioned radio show) and honed their art into a diamond-sharp series of irreverent wonders. In one scene from the show, the two leads sit down and discuss their strategy for the rest of the series, charting out how many hits and how many misses they'll use in each episode—the joke being, no performer plans for a miss: they just happen. But really, that's not a problem Mitchell and Webb seem to have.

Leslie Nielsen in *The Naked Gun: From the Files of Police Squad!* (Photofest © Paramount Pictures)

4

WHAT'S ON THE TELEVISION?

Of course, a Pythonite won't be satisfied with sketch shows alone. Here are some other series you may want to consider.

Doctor Who (1963–1989, 2005–) was never meant to be a comedy show. As such, it's not as easy a fit as some of the other shows and movies in this book. And yet it's a fair assumption that the crossover between Pythonites and Whovians is a substantial one. Part of that is the thorough Britishness of both shows. It seems shallow, but for many Americans, *Flying Circus* seemed to come from a land where smart people prospered by making fun of fools, and *Doctor Who* strengthens this perspective, with a hero who continually triumphs over adversity by essentially being the most overqualified nerd in the history of the universe. The Doctor is clever, resourceful, and he has a time machine. Plus, beautiful women follow him around wherever he goes. What's not to love?

There's a wealth of *Who* for the uninitiated to dive into, and not all of it's good. The show can be roughly divided into two eras. The first era, which ran from 1963 to 1989, told long stories over multiple episodes, with a straightforward, often wry tone that belied its complicated mythology and occasionally bargain-basement alien designs. A possible entry point into this era is one with a familiar face for Pythonites. John Cleese has a cameo in *City of Death* (1979), a serial story that also featured writing work by Douglas Adams (going off a script by David Fisher). *Death* stars the Fourth Doctor, Tom Baker, arguably the most famous performance of the show's title character in the first era, and his companion Romana (Lalla Ward), as they work to stop an alien scheme centered on the theft of the *Mona Lisa* and time travel.

The second era of *Doctor Who*, which showrunner Russell T. Davies initiated in 2005, retains the original show's basic mythology and continuity while giving a new spin to the material, with shorter multi-episode arcs and more standalones. For better and (occasional) worse, modern *Who* puts as much emphasis on emotional investment as it does on science fiction tropes and monsters, presenting its central character as a superhero powered by wisdom and joie de vivre. Anyone looking for a good entry point to these years could safely start from the very beginning, with Christopher Eccleston's debut at the Ninth Doctor in "Rose." Pythonites who worry that the second *Who* era's accessibility means a dumbing down of the show's intelligence might also check out "Blink," the tenth episode of the second era's third series. It features less of the Tenth Doctor (David Tennant) than most episodes of his time on the show, but, without spoiling anything, "Blink" is as thoroughly *Doctor Who* as anything the show ever produced.

Leslie Nielsen started his career as a square-jawed hero type, making his leading-man debut as the square-jawed hero of *Forbidden Planet*. This type lasted him for twenty some odd years, through any number of television and intermittently memorable film roles, until 1977's *Airplane!* teamed him up with Jim Abrams and David and Jerry Zucker. They joined forces again for the short-lived 1982 ABC series ***Police Squad!***, and whatever changes *Airplane!* might have effected on Nielsen's public persona, *Squad* sealed the deal. The square-jaw was now placed in a series of increasingly absurd situations, a straight man in a loopy, slapstick world of visual puns, running gags, and parodies of television convention. Instead of creating a bland hero, Nielsen's stolid delivery made him the perfect center for all the craziness.

Well, perfect may be the wrong word. While Nielsen's great as Frank Drebin, a hero unafraid to run over trash cans or perform stand-up comedy in the name of justice, *Police Squad!* ran only six episodes. This is partly due to ABC's unwillingness to stand be-hind the fledgling series, as its rapid-fire joke delivery and lack of any real sentiment made it an anomaly in the television landscape. But even in its brief run, the strain of packing thirty minutes with enough gags starts to show. Some jokes are repeated each episode (like a shoe-shiner who knows, basically, everything), and while the repetition works well enough, it's easy to see where this could have gotten old. Abrams and the Zuckers (often referred to as ZAZ) would've had to have figured out some way of mining new mate-rial in a hurry, or else the show would have become as formulaic and trite as the cop shows it sought to parody.

Thankfully, the six episodes available on DVD are fresh enough. Not all of the punch lines land, but, as with all ZAZ projects, the pace is quick enough that if you don't like the current joke, wait a minute and a new one will come along. Alan North costars as Captain Ed Hocken (a role George Kennedy would take on for the film series), and Ed Williams (who reprises his role for the films) plays Ted Olson, a scientist with a distinct lack of ethics. Among the show's many recurring bits are the guest stars killed off during the opening credits; a voice-over that announces an episode title completely different from the one on-screen; and a series of riffs on the popular "freeze frame" close out of most TV dramas.

Neil (Nigel Planer) is the perpetually put-upon hippy. Rick (Rik Mayall) is the snotty protestor. Mike (Christopher Ryan) is the cool one. And Vyvyan (Adrian Edmondson) is the punk thug. They're idiots and horrible people to a man, and they all live together in **The Young Ones** (1982–1984), a two-series BBC sitcom that fol-lowed their awful, miserable adventures. It's hard to imagine any of the show's leads surviving long on their own, but together, they are a force of nature whose destructive capabilities are matched only by their inability to accomplish much of anything.

The Young Ones matches *Flying Circus* in its eagerness to tear down the fourth wall, jump from subject to subject seemingly at whim, and reject tradition at every turn. In each slightly-over-half-an-hour-long episode, the four main morons deal with money problems, discarded nuclear weapons, bad television programming, and their own inability to understand what's going on around them. There are musical guests and puppets, and series cowriter Alexei Sayle pops in on occasion to rant at everyone in a Russian accent.

It's rather amazing that the show managed to last as long as it did, because it's an anarchic, free-form explosion of cheery misanthropy, nose-thumbing at authority, and cartoonish violence. Each episode seems balanced on the edge of destroying the actors, set, audience, and everything else with a wild abandon that only makes the jokes that much funnier. Where *Flying Circus* started a revolution with its disregard for convention, *Young Ones* takes that revolution to its logical extremes. At its heart is the most hideous nuclear family ever devised: the four college students who represent extreme takes on the prevalent types of the day, who bond together not out of affection, but for the simple reason that no one else could stand any of them. It'd be depressing if not for the snickering.

If *The Young Ones* represents the Python id at its darkest, **The Muppet Show** (1976–1981) takes that free spirit and creative chaos in a more good-natured direction, with a franchise that represents the best possible definition of "family-friendly entertainment." Created by American puppeteer Jim Henson for the British network ITV, *The Muppet Show* is a playful celebration of bad puns, vaudeville shtick, music, and that old putting-on-a-show spirit. Where *The Young Ones* (and, to an extent, the work of Python itself) was dedicated to the destruction of tired clichés with a barely suppressed contempt, *The Muppet Show* delights in the old and the new, and is childish with the boundless optimism and open heart of youth. Also, there is a pig who does kung fu, and a bear who tells terrible jokes. So it's a rich tapestry.

The series' premise: Kermit the Frog (voiced and manipulated by Henson) is the director in charge of a song-and-dance show that is always about five seconds and a misplaced stick of dynamite away from total collapse. With his best friend Fozzie the Bear (Frank Oz), Kermit has to soothe egos, bury hatchets, and deal with sarcastic audiences. Each week, a new human guest star tries to surf the chaos—luminaries of stage and screen like Steve Martin,

Madeline Kahn, Vincent Price, and Python member John Cleese, among others. But the heart of the series is Kermit, Fozzie, a porcine beauty queen named Miss Piggy (Oz), the whatchamacallit Gonzo the Great (Dave Goelz), the heckling Statler and Waldorf (Richard Hunt and Henson), and the rest.

The term "family friendly" has come to signify bland, toothless pablum—movies and television programs that seek to appease everyone by pleasing no one. It's true that the Muppets don't quite have the edge of Python at its sharpest, but not everything has to be edgy to be funny. Besides, the show does have a certain kind of edge, even if it is buried in felt, with its self-aware characters and frequent explosions. Over the course of five seasons, *The Muppet Show* had a little something for everyone, slapstick and cool monsters for the kids, sophisticated references and amazing puppetry for the grown-ups. And heart, too. Everybody loves heart.

The show was successful enough for the ensemble to make the jump to the big screen during the show's run, with 1979's **The Muppet Movie**. Ostensibly the story of how the Muppets met each other on the road to fame and fortune, *Movie* is really just a string of light sketches and minor tensions, held together in no small part by goodwill and the enthusiasm of its creators. The film slightly tones down the show's wildness and pushes a greater emotional investment in the characters with songs like "The Rainbow Connection," but it's still a sweet, fun romp. More films would follow, like **The Great Muppet Caper** (1981) and **The Muppets Take Manhattan** (1984), and while the franchise wouldn't always reach the heights of its origins, Pythonites would be well advised to have at least some working knowledge of the green frog with the big dreams and his loopy, loony pals.

The antihero is a popular staple of television drama these days, but he's been running amok through television comedy for decades. The English love their antiheroes. On American television, the lead character has to be sympathetic in some fashion for a series to be expected to survive; even Tony Soprano had aspirations of being a better man. For the Brits, though, if he's interesting, that's all that matters. That's not to say **Blackadder** (1983–1989), the titular character of a four-series comedy set in various historical eras, is exactly unlikable. Rowan Atkinson plays a series of descendants who are united by their greed, arrogance, and general contempt for the world of idiots around them. Thing is, the world of *Blackadder is* full of idiots. There's something to be said for following the closest thing to a smart person in the room.

In *The Black Adder*, the first series, set in 1485 and written by Richard Curtis and Atkinson, Edmund, the Duke of Edinburgh who fancies himself as "The Black Adder," conspires to seize power from his father, Richard IV (it's something of an alternate history). The series introduced Atkinson and his loyal servant Baldrick (Tony Robinson), but here, Edmund is a nitwit, generally responsible for the unraveling of his own schemes. It wasn't till the second series, *Blackadder II*, that the character would take the form that would define him for the rest of the run of the show. In *II*, set during the reign of Elizabeth I (1558–1603) and written by Curtis and Ben Elton, Atkinson is Edmund, Lord Blackadder, descendant of the hero of the first series, a cunning, clever son of a bitch with a remarkable gift for insult. For the next three series (*II*; *Blackadder the Third*, which has the character serving as butler to the moronic Prince of Wales; and *Blackadder Goes Forth*, set in the trenches of the First World War), with the eternally incompetent Baldrick at his side, Blackadder would struggle against fools, with only his wits to aid him.

Blackadder is notable for the verbal dexterity of its hero, and for a rotating cast of some of the brightest faces of British comedy, including Hugh Laurie, Stephen Fry, and Miranda Richardson. The best series of the show capture the snotty, snide tone of anyone who has ever been trapped in a position for which he considers himself hopelessly overqualified, held back by the restraints of society's refusal to recognize his greatness. In arguably his best role, Atkinson is the symbol of frustrated ego, a super-genius stuck in the slow class, an outlet for every moment of the day when the perfect insult springs to mind, but we lack the courage to use it. The fact that he might be just as mad as the rest only makes it funnier.

. . .

These days, television sitcoms go out of their way to hide their use of familiar plotlines. Some shows, like *Community*, make the familiarity part of the joke, connecting with their audiences through a shared love of older series; other shows find new ways to tell old stories, like *Modern Family*, which relies on the mockumentary style to liven up some old-fashioned family wackiness. But both these shows maintain the consistency of their own fictional construct. Even when *Community* calls attention to the games it plays, the fourth wall stays in place—Joel McHale never turns to the camera to ask what the audience thinks of how things are going so far, or walks beyond the boundaries of the set to observe the action from afar.

Flying Circus often reminded the viewers at home that they were just that: viewers. But with Python, the stakes were different, because the troupe was rarely interested in anyone caring much what happened to the Spanish Inquisition or the Piranha Brothers. It's arguably more impressive, then, that ***It's Garry Shandling's Show*** (1986–1990) followed the same path; as a situational comedy even more traditional in its setting than most regular '80s shows, *Shandling's Show* made it a point to constantly break down the wall between the actors and the audience, while at the same time relying on an audience having enough affection for the characters and their small world to keep watching.

Garry Shandling stars as, well, Garry Shandling, an insecure stand-up comedian obsessed with getting laid and commenting on his obsession with getting laid. From the start of the first episode, which features Garry moving into his new house and dallying with a starstruck cable girl, Shandling spends as much time talking to the audience as he does to other characters. He references the plot, points out the confines of the set, and, over four seasons and seventy-two episodes, never lets anyone watching forget that she's watching a TV show. It's not always the funniest conceit—the show has its share of good laugh lines (like the theme song, with lyrics like "The song is halfway finished, how do you like it so far?"), but its biggest strength is how easily Shandling's running meta-commentary fits into and enlivens the occasional cliché. Instead of serving as a distraction, the self-reference builds Shandling's connection with the audience; he is, after all, just saying what we're all thinking.

In a way, Shandling's constant deconstruction of his on-screen adventures in *Shandling's Show* mimics the neurotic behavior of a performer constantly questioning his ability to engage with the people around him. The actor would take this concern in a different, less overtly surreal fashion in his next and greatest series, **The Larry Sanders Show** (1992–1998). Airing six seasons on HBO, *Larry Sanders* focuses on the on-camera antics and the behind-the-scenes insecurity of *The Larry Sanders Show*, a fictional late-night talk show along the lines of *The Tonight Show* and *Late Night with David Letterman*. Episodes split their time between showing scenes from the talk show itself, where the host holds court with movie stars and his ever-sycophantic sidekick, and then following the backstage action that makes the talk show possible, where writers squabble, egos fray, and a mighty producer holds sway.

Shandling stars as Sanders, the titular host, a somewhat darker, more neurotic version of his alter ego from *Garry Shandling's Show*. The heart of *Larry Sanders* is Sanders's relationship with his producer, Artie (Rip Taylor), a been-there, done-that super-genius of show business who knows every angle and just how to play them; and his sidekick, Hank Kingsley (Jeffrey Tambor), the raving id to Artie's ego, a desperately needy, perpetually selfish mess of self-pity and greed. The three deal with all the horrors Hollywood has to offer, including power-hungry up-and-comers, social slights, the cost of fame, and double-booked guests. *Larry Sanders* never calls attention to its own fiction in the way *Shandling's Show* did, but it's a more biting, cynical series, full of very clever, very paranoid people always waiting for the other shoe to drop. Both shows are innovative, ahead of their time, and of interest to Pythonites who value honesty as much as laughs.

It's hard to think of a more improbable television success story than **Mystery Science Theater 3000** (1988–1999). Over ten years, three networks, and a whole lot of cast changes, the basic premise remained consistent: a guy stuck on a satellite with his robot friends is forced to watch some of the worst movies ever made, and we get to watch along with them. Watching terrible films isn't everybody's idea of a good time, but *MST3K* does the work of mocking horrible dialogue, cheap effects, and nonsensical plots, as our heroes riff their way through the dregs of cinema, one zipper-suited monster at a time.

Created by Joel Hodgson in 1988, the series has a lot to offer Pythonites. It shares the Python spirit of deconstructive humor, constantly drawing attention to its own absurdities. It also shares the troupe's willingness to indulge in obscure references; there are gags here that won't make sense to anyone who isn't one of the writers, but the obscurity is part of the fun, providing the sense that there are new jokes to discover with each new viewing. *MST3K* can be split into eras: there are the Joel years, when Hodgson hosted, from 1988 to 1993, and the Mike Nelson years, from 1993 to the show's finale in 1999. Each era has its advantages (Joel is more genial, goofy; Mike has a harder edge), but both represent television meta-comedy at its finest. Places to start: *Manos: The Hands of Fate, Eegah!, The Beast of Yucca Flats, Hobgoblins.*

There's something to be said for a commitment to a premise. Most television comedies abandon their initial plot hook a few episodes into their first season, because most television comedies aren't really about plot, at least not in the overarching sense; they deal in setting and character. **Red Dwarf** (created by Rob Grant and Doug Naylor, 1988–1999, 2009, 2012) has both, and it also has one core rule that it's stuck to through its entire run: its protagonist is the last human being in the universe. The show has found ways to get around this via story developments like time warps, alternate realities, and nanotechnology, but while it may seem like drawing a fine line, there's something to be said for never officially cheating on that original concept. Dave Lister (Craig Charles) never just stumbles across a lost human colony that the computer forgot to mention.

For good reason, too. Sometime in the late twenty-second century, the Red Dwarf mining ship suffers a radiation leak that kills nearly the entire crew. The only survivor is Dave Lister, held in cryostasis at the time of the leak. The computer holds Lister in stasis for three million years until radiation levels on the ship decrease, and when Lister emerges from his millennia-long nap, his only on-ship companions are Arnold Rimmer (Chris Barrie), a holographic representation of Lister's former roommate who died during the leak; the Cat (Danny John-Jules), the evolutionary descendant of Lister's house-pet; and Holly (Clare Grogan and Chloe Annett), the ship's onboard computer. Determined not to let his isolated state get him down, Lister sets the ship on a course for Earth and settles into his new job of battling weird biological and space-time threats, and holding on to his sanity.

Red Dwarf succeeds for two reasons: the relationship between Lister, a good-natured slob, and Rimmer, a twerpish, insecure neurotic; and the smart, thoughtful storytelling. Cast chemistry throughout the series is solid, but it's especially strong between Charles and Barrie, and the interplay between them provides much of the humor and, at times, something close to heart. As well, the individual episodes take the science fiction genre of the show seriously, working off concepts that wouldn't seem out of place on a strong episode of *Star Trek*. Monty Python fandom is a nerd calling card, and *Red Dwarf* hits all the classic nerd sweet spots, rewarding intelligence, a passion for continuity, and a love of the stars in equal measure.

The Simpsons (1989–) has been on the air for over twenty years now, an impressive feat for any television series, and one that shouldn't be underrated. Still, it's a shame that in the past decade, the former critical darling has lost a good deal of what made it so successful in the first place, trading in clever, insightful writing and beloved characters for easy pop culture gags and empty cynicism. The modern incarnation isn't a terrible show by any means, but it's hardly essential—and for the first eight seasons of its run, that's exactly what *The Simpsons* was: required viewing for comedy fans and anyone with an interest in well-made TV.

The animated series follows the lives of the Simpson family:

Homer (Dan Castellaneta), father, husband, nuclear power employee, and stand-in for all that's wrong and right about America; Marge (Julie Kavner), devoted housewife, mother, and neat-freak with a stack of blue hair atop her head that was presumably designed by Frank Lloyd Wright; Bart (Nancy Cartwright), the eldest child, son, more menacing than Dennis, with a yen for slingshots and catchphrases; Lisa (Yeardley Smith), the middle child, daughter, super brilliant, more often than not the voice of the family's conscience, with a soft spot for teen idols; and Maggie, the baby girl, who doesn't speak. The family is often at odds with each other over Homer's selfishness, Bart's pranks, Lisa's intellectualism, or other, external causes, but they stick together, because that's what families do.

Originally developed by Matt Groening, *The Simpsons* started life as a series of crudely animated shorts on *The Tracey Ullman* show before debuting as its own series. The first season is better quality than the shorts, but the animation is still on the sluggish side. Also, these initial episodes are from a show still working towards its own unique voice and rely more on standard sitcom plots than do later seasons. The series and the characters come into better focus in the second season, and by the third, *The Simpsons* had found its voice. For the next few years, the show's wild popularity allowed one of the greatest writing staffs on television the creative freedom they needed to make their own particular brand of mad whimsy. Episodes like "Marge vs. the Monorail," "Last Exit to Springfield," and "Cape Feare" managed to blend cartoonish flights of fancy with grounded relationships, and while those relationships would eventually dissolve under the weight of sloppy writing and repetitive gags, those first eight seasons remain an untouched high-water mark in the history television. (The show also inspired *The Simpsons Movie* in 2007.)

It's easy to dismiss the daytime talk show host as the lowest level of media personality, someone who has built a career based on asking empty questions and then pretending the answers are the most fascinating words in the world. But it takes talent to be entertainingly personable with a variety of strangers, and it takes even more talent to keep one's cool whenever something goes wrong. Oprah Winfrey demonstrated the power of the format when she connected with her audiences, but even the most clichéd and hackneyed host has to have some basic charisma and knack for facilitating dialogue.

Enter Alan Partridge, a man who shows just how badly one can fail at being blandly charming. Steve Coogan's arrogant, awkward, hapless Partridge is the host of **Knowing Me Knowing You with Alan Partridge**, a satirical interview program that ran for seven episodes on the BBC in 1994. The character is a carryover from a radio show Coogan did in 1994, and he may even top Ricky Gervais's David Brent in the field of cringe humor catalysts. Partridge is self-absorbed, irritable, and possessed of a faith in his abilities as an entertainer that is thoroughly unfounded in reality. As a host, he's lecherous, pushy, and easily flustered whenever an interview goes off the rails.

Which is unfortunate, because each episode of *Knowing Me* unfolds like a nightmare with a laugh track. In addition to Partridge's general ineptitude, the guests who appear on the program run the gamut from tedious to idiotic, with all the shades of awfulness that come in between. It's hard to believe that even a great host would have been able to manage lewd French mimes, entitled Hollywood brats, and a washed-up movie star power couple. But Partridge somehow finds a way to make even the most uncomfortable confrontations just a little bit worse. Pythonites will appreciate Coogan's fearless willingness to commit to a joke and his ability to poke holes in the pomposity of showbiz suck-ups and talentless hacks alike. All seven episodes of the series are available on DVD.

Anyone who ran a television program as badly as Alan Partridge ran his interview show couldn't expect to stay on the air for very long. Steve Coogan's signature creation was a snobbish, closed-minded nitwit who couldn't conduct a watchable interview if his career depended on it. Which, unfortunately, it did; in the fictional world of *Knowing Me*, network execs canned Partridge's show after its regrettable first season. But Partridge is such an effective, hilarious role for Coogan that a sequel was inevitable. The trick would be to find a way to bring Partridge back on the airwaves without completely violating the plausibility of his fictional world.

The answer? **I'm Alan Partridge** (1997, 2002), a two-series, twelve-episode show about Alan Partridge's doomed struggles to get back to the career for which he is profoundly unsuited. Forced to abandon television, Alan is back on the radio that was his original home, deejaying during a graveyard shift in Norwich. This setback hasn't stunted his ambition, however, and with the help of a much-suffering assistant, Lynn Benfield (Felicity Montagu), Alan is determined to force his way back to the top. Partridge endures much-deserved humiliation at the hands of the staff of the hotel he calls home, scrabbles for hosting work, and struggles to hold on to personal assistants he can in no way justify.

The structure of *Knowing Me* made for a sort of Sartreian claustrophobia for its cast, as Partridge had no place to escape from the confines of the stage. *I'm Alan Partridge* opens things up some, but Coogan retains his gift for constructing painfully embarrassing situations for his despicable leading man. A sequel that works as both a continuation of its predecessor's story and an entity entirely its own, *Partridge* manages to make the continuous assault on its protagonist's ego surprising, hilarious, and strangely gratifying. So many real-world Alan Partridges have risen to ill-deserved fame. It's fun to see one suffer so perpetually for his sins.

Monty Python was never afraid of taking shots at the church, and one of their more memorable sketches starred Terry Jones as "The Bishop," a tough-talking, crime-fighting clergyman. The Bishop sketch had only one joke: theme music blaring, Jones arrives on the scene of an elaborate homicide, always moments too late to save any lives. It's a good gag, made better by gusto, but it doesn't make for much of a character. Still, with a little fleshing out, the Bishop would fit right into the world of **Father Ted** (1995–1998), Graham Linehan (*Black Books*, *The IT Crowd*) and Arthur Mathews' Irish sitcom about a trio of priests banished to a small coastal island. In a land of green pastures and perpetual inconvenience, Jones's Bishop would barely raise an eyebrow.

Over three series and twenty-five episodes, *Ted* paints a picture of a rural community just a few beads short of a rosary. As Father Ted Crilly, Dermot Morgan is the closest thing to sane in the zip code, a perpetually beleaguered man of God who isn't above the occasional moral lapse. It's hard to judge him too harshly for his meager sins, though, considering what he has to endure. Most notably, there are his two compatriots in exile: Father Dougal McGuire (Ardal O'Hanlon), a well-meaning but dimwitted young man with a tendency towards the literal; and Father Jack Hackett (Frank Kelly), a half-mad drunk who speaks largely in growls and curses. Along with their housekeeper, Mrs. Doyle (Pauline McLynn), the three endure all manner of oddness and unwanted guests.

Ted is a sort of lighthearted dark comedy, where one-off characters occasionally drive off cliffs to their deaths without breaking the sitcom surface. Ted and friends go on disastrous vacations, protest filthy movies only to make them more popular than before, and compete in celebrity lookalike contests, among any number of other adventures. The tone is broad, but the performances (particularly Morgan, who plays the "sane man one step over the edge" that Jason Bateman would later adopt for *Arrested Development*) and setting keep the jokes from being too over-the-top. It's an inventive, charming show about how not to lose your mind in the middle of nowhere.

Workplace sitcoms are a dime a dozen, but the best ones realize that colleagues at an office can form their own sketch comedy team: the writing isn't as good, and the only people laughing are the janitors, but the relationships, catchphrases, and prank wars are all just a series of bits designed to get everyone through the day. ***NewsRadio*** (1995–1999) is one of the best examples of this genre, a show with an absurdist sense of humor that will make Pythonites feel right at home. For five seasons, the news team at WYNX dispensed traffic tips, weather reports, sports coverage, and entirely legitimate personal commentary, and they held it together with cheap sarcasm, prop humor, and something occasionally approaching mutual affection.

Created by Paul Simms, a former writer for *The Larry Sanders Show*, *NewsRadio* starts with naive Midwesterner Dave Nelson (Dave Foley) taking over as news director of multimillionaire Jimmy James's (Stephen Root) news station. Dave is going to have his hands full. The station's co-anchor, Bill McNeal (Phil Hartman), is a showboating, egomaniacal buffoon; Catherine Duke (Khandi Alexander), the other co-anchor, who gives as good as she gets; Dave's secretary, Beth (Vicki Lewis), is energetic but kind of a ditz; reporter Matthew Brock (Andy Dick) is a twitchy, incompetent dork; the handyman, Joe Garrelli (Joe Rogan), is a UFO conspiracy nut; and Lisa Miller (Maura Tierney), the most competent professional at the station, is gunning for Dave's job. Fortunately, Dave and Lisa start dating after the first episode of the first season, which takes some of the pressure off, but it's doubtful this solution will work for everyone.

For its first four seasons, *NewsRadio* offered some of the best-crafted workplace comedy on television, with a writing team that understood how to comment on cliché at the same time as they embraced it. Having honed his charisma and comic timing for years on *The Kids in the Hall*, Dave Foley makes a perfect leading man: reasonable, patient and sane, right up until the point where he can't take it anymore. The rest of the cast is equally terrific, and the main reason the fifth season doesn't work as well as the previous four is Phil Hartman's absence; Hartman died in 1998, and in its last year the series acknowledged his death and cast Jon Lovitz as a replacement anchor who never quite managed to fit in. But those first four seasons are top-notch, with great guest stars and a likable, welcoming world. You don't have to love your work to get by, but you take entertainment where you can find it.

The Pythons made a career out of mixing high and low humor, their sketches jumping from high-concept cleverness to slapstick without bothering to distinguish much between the two. Anything for a laugh was the point, which meant that any good gag was worth using, whether or not it made the audience think. The animated series **Futurama** isn't quite so mercenary in its scripting; unlike *Flying Circus*, the show has recurring characters and, more

importantly, wants the audience to have some emotional investment in those characters. But in terms of jokes, it takes the same
wide-ranging approach, which means that lines about defecating in
wastebaskets can sit side by side with quips about the Uncertainty
Principle. It's the sort of show that regularly rewards you for being
smart, while not discounting the lizard-brain appeal of stupidity.

Philip J. Fry (Billy West) was never all that great a pizza delivery man, and on the eve of 2000, he's in a bit of a rut—his girlfriend has just dumped him, and his latest delivery call is a prank
that sends him to a cryogenics lab, where Fry inadvertently (or so it
would seem) falls into one of the freezers, only to wake up a thousand years later. The year 3000 is much like today, although there
are boozing robots, one-eyed love interests, human-sized lobster
doctors, and mad scientists with an unfortunate tendency to fall
asleep midsentence. But Fry is determined to make the most of it,
even if that includes space wasps, Slurm factories, and selling his
hands to the Robot Devil.

Futurama was created by *Simpsons* creator Matt Groening and developed by Groening and David X. Cohen. It originally ran for five seasons (1999–2003); then fan outcry at its cancellation prompted four
feature-length episodes, produced for DVD, and ultimately brought
the show back to the air in 2010. In addition to West, who provides
multiple voices on the show, the voice cast features Joe DiMaggio,
Katey Sagal, Maurice LaMarche, Lauren Tom, Phil Lamarr, and
Tress MacNeille. It's a black comedy, science fiction adventure action farce, capable of painfully strong emotional gut punches, and
it's wickedly funny when it's at its best, which is frequently.

One of the hallmarks of the true Pythonite is an ability to reference lines from Python routines on demand. Quoting routines is a
form of paying homage to a beloved sketch, while at the same time
hoping that some of the energy and humor of the original writing
will rub off on you. But even more than that, repeating Python
sketches to other fans is a way of sharing appreciation and creating an instant connection between strangers. You may not know
the guy next to you from Adam, but if you can both throw out the

Argument Clinic sketch without breaking a sweat, well, you've got something in common from the start. The characters of **Spaced** (1999–2001), the two-series British comedy show directed by Edgar Wright, don't share all the same points of interest, but they have enough to get by. Even more importantly, Wright, along with series writers and costars Simon Pegg and Jessica Stevenson, recognized that pop culture references can help bond an audience to their heroes, making the figures on the screen seem more real than they otherwise might be.

Pegg and Stevenson play Tim and Daisy, a pair of twentysomethings without much direction in life who find themselves in need of a place to live. They find the perfect flat, but the ad placed by the landlady, the wine-loving, middle-aged Marsha (Julia Deakin), specifies "professional couples only." So, in classic sitcom style, Tim and Daisy pretend they're lovers, even though they really aren't, even if they're totally perfect for each other. Over fourteen episodes, the two will struggle with bad breakups, career ennui, and general young-adult angst, while building an inadvertent family with their housemates and close friends.

Spaced helped solidify the comedic partnership of Wright, Pegg, and Nick Frost (who appears as Pegg's best friend Mark), a trio that would pay off well on the big screen in the years to come, but the series itself is reward enough. There's drama and many of the usual misunderstandings that drive the situational comedy, but the general tone of the show is that of manic sensibility combined with affable geniality. The enthusiasm of everyone involved rings through every episode. The pop culture nods could've been exclusionary—"Ha-ha, we've seen this, you haven't"—but play instead as gleeful tribute and are a welcome to anyone who's ever broken the ice by shouting "Ni!" in a crowded room.

People aren't always that fun to deal with. Especially customers; they're whiny and needy, and the cash they offer in exchange for the goods provided is never a sufficient reward for the time lost in satisfying their petty whims. At least, that's the attitude of Bernard Black (Dylan Moran), owner and proprietor of the titular book store in **Black Books** (2000–2004), a British sitcom about the perils of retail and the horrors of daily life in a world full of strangers. Along with his assistant Manny Bianco (Bill Bailey) and his friend Fran Katzenjammer (Tamsin Greig), Bernard navigates his occasional encounters with the outside world with a barely concealed indifference and contempt.

Which, clearly, is something that Pythonites can identify with. As created by Moran and Graham Linehan (*Father Ted, Big Train, The IT Crowd*), *Books* is at heart a sitcom that follows the same structures as many American shows; there are plots here that wouldn't be out of place on an episode of *Seinfeld*, like one where Fran keeps hounding a man she doesn't particularly like (played by Peter Serafinowicz) because his voice helps her get off. But the one-liners are well-written, and the chemistry of the main cast helps some familiar story arcs seem fresh. *Books* doesn't make the mistake of siding with Bernard's essential misanthropy, but it still finds a lot of entertainment value in watching him bounce off the unsuspecting masses. *Books* ran for three series, a total of eighteen episodes. Python fans will appreciate its wit and recognize the unspoken truth that reading is better than talking to anyone, nine times out of ten.

On the whole, *Monty Python* never much went in for cringe humor; sketch comedy rarely does. "Cringe humor" gets its name from the reaction it inspires in its audience, a mixture of wincing at the embarrassment on screen and laughter at the awful absurdity of events. Sketches, which don't generally encourage any kind of emotional investment or even much more than shallow empathy for their characters, aren't really capable of the kind of attachment required to make this work. Besides, the straight men in *Flying Circus* sketches are often just as silly as the loonies they're forced to deal with. (Brian in *Life of Brian* may be the closest thing to a sympathetic hero the troupe ever created, but even then, the situations he encounters aren't ever that hard to watch.)

For the real master class in how to wring the most embarrassment and nervous chuckles out of a situation, one need only watch Ricky Gervais and Stephen Merchant's **The Office** (2001–2003), a two-series show that runs twelve episodes, plus two Christmas specials. The premise: a never-seen documentary film crew is shooting footage in a paper company in Slough, England. The crew is making a movie about a workplace, but they inadvertently manage to find the office with perhaps the worst boss in the history of bad bosses: David Brent, played by Gervais.

Brent is weaselly, desperate for attention, convinced he's an entertainer when he's awful at performance, childish, petulant, vindictive, and cruel. And he makes the lives of the people who work for him an endless series of meaningless humiliations. Tim (Martin Freeman) and Dawn (Lucy Davis) are the nominal normal people who try to maintain their sanity in the face of the daily grind; Gareth (Mackenzie Crook) is Brent's militant, nerdy second-in-command. Partly *The Office* is about just how miserable a job can be and still be the only thing you've got going, and partly it's about two people who may or may not be the perfect match, but mostly, it's about the sweating, smirking, humiliating awkwardness that is David Brent, and how a simple conversation—or, say, an ill-advised dance-off—can be harder to watch than even the goriest on-screen murder. Not to be missed.

It'd be fairly easy to separate the modern sitcom into two basic conceptual types: on the one hand, you have the traditional comedies, ones that use familiar tropes with maybe a wink and a nod to the audience, but are still played fairly straight; and on the other hand, you've got the shows that actively work to deconstruct those tropes. (Or maybe you could just say all shows are on a curve, starting with *The Honeymooners* and ending with *It's Garry Shandling's Show*.) However you look at it, **Arrested Development** (2003–2006) is nearly as meta as it gets. Running for three seasons, this low-rated cult classic took a wacky premise—a sane man trying to protect his crazy family—and stretched it in every possible direction, creating the sort of intricate, wickedly clever show that was born to be watched and re-watched on DVD for years to come.

Jason Bateman stars as Michael Bluth, the son of George Bluth, Sr. (Jeffrey Tambor), and the only Bluth who's anything close to a rational adult. When the senior Bluth is arrested, Michael steps in to run the Bluth Corporation and to try and bring some order to the Bluth clan: his arrogant, icy mother Lucille (Jessica Walter), spoiled princess sister Lindsay (Portia de Rossi), and idiot magician brother, George "Gob" Bluth II (Will Arnett). As well, he's got to take care of his son, George Michael (Michael Cera), who's somehow fallen in love with his cousin, Maeby (Alia Shawkat), the daughter of Lindsay and her husband, Tobias Funke (David Cross.) Then there's the legacy his father left for him to unravel, occasional appearances by George Sr.'s twin brother (also played by Tambor), and a host of guest stars, plot twists, and running gags.

Those running gags are a key part of *Development*'s effectiveness, actually. This is a layered show, of the sort where it really is possible to notice a new pop culture riff or resonance every time you watch an episode, and the running gags are a way of tying everything together, like repeated motifs. Michael (who, in one of the show's best jokes, isn't quite as sane as he likes to think he is) is constantly struggling with his commitment to his family, and there's just enough sincerity in there, especially in Michael's relationship with his son, to keep the series from descending into complete nihilism; but there's little in the way of sentimentality in the show—or, at least, sentiment that isn't immediately undercut by absurdity. All three seasons are available on disc; Python fans will enjoy the smart writing and self-referential humor, as well as some absolutely top-notch performances.

On the animated action-adventure-satire **The Venture Brothers** (2003–), struggling scientist and grown-up Boy Adventurer Rusty Venture (voiced by James Urbaniak) is kind of a jerk. He spends his time scrambling for cash, endangering the lives of his sons Hank (Christopher McCulloch) and Dean (Michael Sinterniklaas), throwing himself at women who don't want him, and fending off the advances of his sometime arch-nemesis, The Monarch (McCulloch). But it's hard not to feel bad for Rusty; his father, a hard-living super-genius from a time when men did science first, asked questions later, destroyed his childhood and left him ill prepared to face an adult world where "adventuring" usually amounts to filling out your tax forms properly.

Besides, the world Daddy Venture left behind doesn't really provide much room for character growth. As created by Jackson Publick (a pseudonym of McCulloch's), *Venture Brothers* started as a satire of *Johnny Quest*–style shows, starring Rusty, his sons, and their occasionally psychotic bodyguard Brock Samson (Patrick Warburton). But in the years since it premiered, the series has broadened its aim, expanding its mythology in order to create a world populated by near misses in spandex, power-hungry madmen, and homoerotic super-soldiers. It's a world of people who use the pageantry of superhero costumes and pulp story theatrics to escape from hollow lives.

Which isn't to say that *Venture* is a depressing series. McCulloch and writing partner Doc Hammer don't shy away from misery, but the show also regularly acknowledges that the reason all these comic book shenanigans maintain their appeal is that, pathetic or not, they're a lot of fun. The show's sharp dialogue, obscure references, and strong sense of character have kept it running long past the point where the initial concept ran out of steam. It's a show for nerds that accepts the uglier aspects of actually being a social outcast, and Pythonites will find much to like here.

As high concepts go, ***Garth Marenghi's Darkplace*** (2004), a British series that aired on Channel 4 in 2004, is a doozy. Cocreated by Matthew Holness and Richard Ayoade, *Garth Marenghi's Darkplace* stars Holness as Garth Marenghi, a famous horror novelist (somewhat reminiscent of Stephen King) who created a show called *Darkplace* for British television in the 1980s. The show, which featured copious violence, unsettling imagery, and horrible, horrible acting, never aired, but now Marenghi is bringing it to light for his fans, along with interviews with the cast as they reminisce over a misbegotten project they are all firmly convinced was the high point of their meager artistic careers.

Got that? It's a show . . . within a show . . . within a show. While this may sound thoroughly baffling in description, in practice, it's a wonderfully effective simultaneous satire of awful genre television and the ego-stroking puff pieces that so often accompany those shows in retrospectives. Words can't adequately convey the delight of seeing a man give birth to an eyeball baby or a hospital beset by malevolent Scotsmen, and all six episodes are jammed full of movie riffs, clunky line readings, and ridiculous effects. Ayoade appears on-screen as Marenghi's producer/costar Dean Lerner, and fans of *The IT Crowd* will also recognize Matt Berry as the vainglorious Todd Rivers; Alice Lowe rounds out the cast as the hapless Madeline Wool.

Darkplace only ran a single series; it's best to start from the beginning and watch all six episodes in order. The show works hard to parody as many horror clichés as possible, as Marenghi the writer clearly never met an idea he couldn't copy. Over the course of its brief run, the show managed to create its own distinct mythology—the cast interviews make it obvious that Madeline Wool has disappeared since *Darkplace* originally aired, with the implication that Lerner may have done something to her. Her fate may never be resolved; given that the first series aired seven years ago, those six episodes will most likely be all the world ever gets of the show. But with a concept this unusual, maybe it's for the best that *Darkplace* never got a chance to get old.

There is something undeniably childish about the work of Monty Python. Indeed, three members of the group (Eric Idle, Michael Palin, and Terry Jones) worked on a children's show, *Do Not Adjust Your Set*, before joining with the others to open the *Flying Circus*. The troupe's particular brand of irreverence always had an undercurrent of an adolescent thumbing his nose at his elders just because he could. Something of this spirit informs **The Mighty Boosh**. A comedy troupe that began as a stage show and radio series, *Boosh* came to British television in 2004, running for three series, a total of twenty-one episodes, for one of the strangest comedies / musical puppet shows this side of the Muppets. Probably stranger than the Muppets, even, as Kermit never headlined an electro-funk band, or fought against a demonic, world-threatening nana.

It's difficult to describe *Boosh* precisely. The show follows the adventures of Howard Moon (Julian Barratt), a deeply uncool buffoon with a love for all things square, and his best friend, Vince Noir (Noel Fielding), a glam-rock hipster who isn't quite as cool as he thinks he is. They play music together, work at a zoo for a while, and hang out with Naboo (Michael Fielding), a mystical shaman with an ape familiar named Bollo. There are crazy creatures, and magic, and monsters, and funky songs (written by Baratt). It all sort of makes sense as it goes, but retains the quality of a fever dream brought on by an overdose of Nyquil, Skittles, and H.R. Pufnstuf.

Boosh isn't really a show for kids, as it has its share of frank sexual material, but it *looks* like it should be, which is clearly by design. Modern comedy in the last decade or so has done its best to combine the surreal lunacy of childhood with adult concerns, to varying degrees of success, but *Boosh* hits the mark more often than not. The show creates a world in which seemingly anything can happen, but still manages to operate on its own internal logic so that even the most random developments (like a musician with a door in his hair) don't seem entirely random. Pythonites should enjoy its silliness, wit, and the Moon/Noir dynamic, which mimics classic vaudevillian routines.

Nerds aren't often treated well by popular culture. Admittedly, a certain portion of that culture is given over entirely to nerd-centric obsessions, but whenever a smart, somewhat unphotogenic, socially awkward individual (nearly always male) arrives in a movie or TV show, that individual is nearly always venal, immature, and incapable of performing even the most basic real-world task without collapsing in terror. ***The IT Crowd*** (2006–) isn't entirely guiltless of this. Its two male leads, Roy Trenneman (Chris O'Dowd) and Maurice Moss (Richard Ayoade), are computer geeks with poor conversational skills, an interest in video games, and a complete inability to talk to women. Which makes life a trifle difficult for Jen Barber (Katherine Parkinson), their somewhat computer-illiterate boss—who is, being a woman, better adjusted, interested in shoes, etc.

But hey, some jokes are familiar because they're true, and *The IT Crowd* works because, familiar or not, its characters are a bit more than just types. The show wrings the most it can from a fish-out-of-water sitcom premise: one day, Jen somehow fakes her way into a job as the head of an IT department. This upsets Roy, who feels his territory being encroached upon, and doesn't matter all that much to Maurice, and a bit of squabbling ensues. This would get tiresome quickly, and fortunately isn't really what the show is about. There are the occasional pranks and feuds, but the trio learn soon that they could use each other's help; the men because they need a normal person to give them advice, and Jen because, well, she likes having a job, and deep down, she's probably just as nerdy as the rest of them.

Pythonites will enjoy *The IT Crowd* as a sitcom that does a lot of the standard sitcom things (there are episodes about misunderstandings, awkward situations, and relationship difficulties) but provides just enough geeky jokes to bridge the gap between conventional TV and more cult-oriented fare. It's smart but not groundbreaking, clever but doesn't try to reinvent the form. In essence, it's a pleasant show, with just a dash of unique flavor.

Comedy is a form of shock. Usually that shock is a benign one, but Monty Python was never afraid to go for the jugular when it wanted to. Take the Mr. Creosote sketch from *The Meaning of Life*. Terry Jones plays a grotesquely overweight man who dines at a fancy restaurant. At the encouragement of snooty waiter John Cleese, Creosote eats and eats and eats, occasionally vomiting into a bucket when the mood takes him, and it's gross. Very, very gross. The punch line is even grosser: Cleese pushes a "wafer-thin mint" on the fat man, he eats it, and then he explodes. It's not that funny a gag, and, despite Cleese's over-the-top snideness, it doesn't really play as funny either.

The sketch is more about the gross-out, comedy as a form of guerrilla theater that works to get under the viewer's skin, earning laughter that serves as a defense mechanism against discomfort. In this way, it's a clear ancestor of the work of Tim Heidecker and Eric Wareheim on their series ***Tim and Eric Awesome Show, Great Job!*** (2007–2010). The five-season show leveled assaults against good taste, decency, and the accepted standards for sketch comedy, one eleven-minute episode at a time. The premise, as much as there is one, is a series of ads, public domain programs, and news from Channel 5. The show has had a wide variety of guest stars, including Michael Cera, David Cross, Ben Stiller, Alan Thicke, and Ray Wise, among many, many others. John C. Reilly has a recurring role as the woefully inept science reporter personality Dr. Steve Brule, who got a spin-off in 2010's *Check It Out! with Steve Brule*.

Awesome Show isn't as immediately accessible as many of the shows and movies referenced in this book, and it's not really for everyone. Heidecker and Wareheim's form of comedy is aggressive, unsettling, and often nightmarish, and that's the point: Monty Python managed to blend popular sentiment with the cutting edge, but true Pythonites are as interested in fringe humor as they are in the mainstream. *Awesome Show* highlights the desperate, the deluded, and the sweaty, cringing freak without ever openly admitting their strangeness, treating every damp brow and awful smile with unblinking focus and something curiously close to compassion. It's not always the most pleasant viewing, but it's distinctive, and worth seeing at least once. Just don't expect a lot of punch lines.

Whatever underlying principles and revolutionary approach the Monty Python troupe brought to its work, the simple fact is, the group wrote and performed in sketches and films to make people laugh. In this, they share much in common with the makers of ***Archer*** (2009–), an animated spy spoof whose primary purpose is to get as many jokes as possible out of a group of malcontents, spoiled brats, and sexual deviants. With two seasons already under its belt and a third on the way, *Archer* doesn't much go in for emotional depth or social relevance, and while the show dabbles in multi-episode arcs and maintains its own mythology, all of that works towards making it a more effective humor delivery device.

If this makes *Archer* sound shallow, it shouldn't. Unlike, say,

Family Guy, which gets most of its comedic mileage out of simple juxtaposition and regurgitation, *Archer* is a smart, often wickedly cynical show that uses a solid base of well-drawn characters for its humor. H. Jon Benjamin voices the show's nominal leading man, Sterling Archer, a James Bond type who globe-trots, seduces women, and steals state secrets for ISIS, a freelance espionage agency run by his mother, Malory Archer (Jessica Walter). Sterling is not exactly a role model. He drinks, screws, and fumbles through life like an overgrown boy with severe mommy issues; his only brief moments of competence are found when his life is threatened. And even then, he gets by on a lot of luck.

Not that the rest of ISIS is much better adjusted. Malory is an alcoholic who uses the service as a way to meet rich men, and the support staff (including characters voiced by Judy Greer, Chris Parnell, Amber Nash, and Lucky Nates) is made up of the previously mentioned malcontents, spoiled brats, and sexual deviants. About the only competent character in the bunch is Lana Kane (Aisha Tyler), ISIS's other active agent in the field. Archer travels the globe, fights foreign intrigue, defends young women from assassins, and treats nearly everyone in his life horribly. Benjamin's performance and the cast chemistry ensure that *Archer* is never boring or angsty. It mixes deep-cut references, trusting its audience in the same way Python always did, with occasional violence and broken relationships. And it's funny as hell.

One of the defining qualities of modern comedy is its self-awareness. Jokes aren't always just jokes anymore; sometimes, they're jokes that attempt to derive humor from the fact that audience knows that the writers know that the performer knows he or she is delivering a joke. It sounds a bit complicated, and it can be *very* complicated, but that doesn't make it any less effective. The cast and crew of **Community** know how effective a good meta joke can be, and they also know that meta needs a core of emotional truth to keep working over time. Which translates to a crazy, whip-smart American TV series that rewards its viewers for their commitment and time—much like a certain *Flying Circus*.

Debuting in 2009 on NBC, *Community* stars Joel McHale as Jeff, a lawyer forced to go to Greendale Community College when a judge discovers his lack of actual credentials. At Greendale, Jeff meets Britta (Gillian Jacobs), an attractive fellow student who sees right through Jeff's cheesy seduction attempts. In order to impress her, Jeff puts together a study group including Abed (Danny Pudi), a pop culture savant; Troy (Donald Glover), a well-meaning former jock; Annie (Alison Brie), a high-strung overachiever; Shirley (Yvette Brown), a mother of two trying to get a handle on her life; and Pierce (Chevy Chase), an old rich guy without much of a social filter. Together, the group bonds, goes on adventures, and occasionally attempts to pass their classes.

The premise isn't all that inspired (it sounds like a movie Chase might have starred in three decades ago), but thankfully, the premise is junked almost immediately. Much as *Flying Circus* parodied the pop culture conventions of its time, *Community* riffs on movies, sitcom tropes, and genres with gleeful abandon. But whereas the Pythons were more than willing to sacrifice anything in the name of laughs, *Community*'s creator, Dan Harmon, maintains a core of affection for the show's characters, which makes it more than just a series of sketches. After two seasons, the series has demonstrated a willingness to experiment without ever losing sight of the characters who make it work.

Monty Python's work is about a good many things, most of them quite silly, but one of the troupe's major themes is failure. Failure is big in comedy, as most jokes are based around a character trying to achieve a goal and being blocked in his or her aims, by either an inability to communicate or a refusal by other characters to allow the lead to get what he or she wants. But Python perfected the art. In their best film, *Life of Brian*, the hero really just wants to be a good man and maybe get laid, but instead finds himself dragged into dysfunctional rebellions and idiot politics. The ensemble of **Party Down** (2009–2010) may not suffer from quite the level of physical stress that Brian does, but they understand very well the fine art of getting let down.

The twenty-episode, two-season show tells the story of a group of caterers working for the Party Down company, providing food and fun to LA's rich and famous. The joke being, the caterers are a lot of aspiring writers and actors who still consider their current jobs temporary holdovers until they can start doing what they *really* want to be doing. Adam Scott stars as Henry Pollard, an erstwhile actor best known for his delivery of a slogan in a beer commercial. *State* alumni Ken Marino plays Ron Donald, boss of the group, who dreams of opening his own cracker franchise, and Lizzy Caplan is Casey Klein, Henry's possible love interest, an aspiring comic actress stuck in a frustrated marriage and perpetually on the verge of her big break.

Together with the rest of the cast (Ryan Hansen, Martin Starr, Jane Lynch in the first season, Megan Mullally in the second), the Party Down team struggles with bad bosses, worse luck, and their own sensitive egos. Humiliation comedy is nothing new, but *Party* manages to create a blend of agony and sincerity that makes it stand out from the herd, laughing at its leads while recognizing the real pain that comes from reaching for your dreams and coming up short every time. Created by John Enbom, Rob Thomas, Dan Etheridge, and Paul Rudd, the series mixes farce, slapstick, and cringe in equal measure, never softening its blows and earning every brief moment of sentiment.

Honesty may not be the first adjective that comes to mind when trying to describe the work of Monty Python, but it's applicable enough. All the best comedy stems, in some way or another, from telling the truth, especially if that truth comes from an awkward or ridiculous place. And if you're looking for awkward and ridiculous, there are few better places to search than the *Flying Circus*. Still, Python never went in for anything deeper than "The world is pretty goddamn ridiculous, eh?" For anyone looking to get a glimpse of the cutting edge of honesty in comedy, and for an example of a modern artist willing to push the television format to the same extremes that Python once did, the work of Louis C.K. is a good place to start.

Louis started his career as a stand-up and writer for shows like *The Late Show with David Letterman, Late Night with Conan O'Brien*, and, briefly, *The Dana Carvey Show*. He's recorded a number of stand-up shows, including **Shameless** (2006), **Chewed-Up** (2008), and **Hilarious** (2010). As a performer, C.K. mixes a confessional style and a brutal directness, telling stories in a low-key, conversational tone about the biological horrors of being a middle-aged man, the awkwardness of raising kids, the psychic agony of a failing marriage, and, in general, the myriad humiliations and failures required just to get through the day alive. It doesn't sound like the most chuckle-worthy material, but C.K. manages to get laughs out of even the bleakest of concepts. It's a fearlessness that never proclaims itself; there's never a sense that the performer is trying to draw your attention to his bravery in talking about things no one likes to talk about. Instead, C.K. talks about his life as a man perpetually amazed by the world around him, beaten down by the struggles of existence, but never truly defeated.

The best expression of this approach is in C.K.'s currently airing television show, **Louie** (2010–). The stand-up shows are terrific, but Pythonites should pay particular attention to *Louie*, as it continues the *Flying Circus* tradition of poking around the edges and finding new ways to tell the jokes. *Louie* follows C.K., playing himself, as he goes about his daily business, raising two daughters, hanging out with friends, and facing his own mortality. Each episode features two or three long-form vignettes structured loosely around a common theme, connected by scenes of C.K. doing his stand-up routine at a nightclub. The show is sometimes unsettling, occasionally depressing, often surprisingly beautiful, and quite simply like nothing else on TV. The best episodes capture the feeling of a late-night conversation with an old friend—the laughs aren't always easy to find, but the ones that do come are powerful, affecting, and richly life-affirming.

Peter Boyle and Madeline Kahn in Mel Brooks' *Young Frankenstein*.
(20th Century-Fox Pictures/Photofest © 20th Century-Fox)

5

AT THE MOVIES

Of course, you can't watch television all the time. If thirty-minute blocks are starting to wear you down, you may want to consider the following, a sampling of some of the best cinema has to offer in the true Pythonite style.

There's no denying *Dr. Strangelove* is a dark film, but it's not a particularly uncomfortable one to watch; the characters are so absurd, and the circumstances so far removed from day-to-day reality, that it's easy to feel detached from them. It's not so easy to approach Stanley Kubrick's 1971 film ***A Clockwork Orange*** with the same distance, although it seems like it should be. Adapted from a science fiction novel by Anthony Burgess, *Orange* takes place in a futuristic England, where hooligans run the streets in fancy clothes, and society at large has settled into a comfortable but ill-defined decay. But the rawness of the film's violence and the unsettling conjunction of humor with awful acts can be difficult to watch.

And yet *Orange* is arguably Kubrick's most entertaining film, due in no small part to the terrifying charisma of its leading man. Malcolm McDowell stars as Alex, a juvenile delinquent with a Napoleon complex and taste for classical music. He spends his nights beating up homeless men, stealing, and breaking into strangers' houses to rape their wives, along with his two "droogs" (their slang word for "guys who like to accompany me when I murder, rape, and assault people"). Then one day, Alex's droogs betray him to the police, and Alex goes to jail for his crimes, where he hears of a special new treatment that could win him an early release. It involves watching some movies and taking some drugs, and it's certain to make him a better man.

Orange's unique mixture of snide commentary, ultraviolence, and philosophy will appeal to anyone with an interest in challenging cinema. But Pythonites should find special appeal here because, in a way, Alex represents a possible endpoint to the troupe's anarchic new form of comedy. In his world, Alex is a vile, hateful, destructive twerp, but the people surrounding him are nearly as despicable, and Alex's vitality, charm, and intelligence make him stand above the crowd. Monty Python represented a new youth whose primary interest in sacred cows was making the best possible hamburgers, and while *Orange* is too complex to be simply a paranoid response to that anarchy, it does ask some pointed questions about where all that energy comes from; and how, in our quest to hermetically seal our society against evil, it's possible to forget that sometimes "evil" is just a rough form of change.

Peter O'Toole is a very convincing actor. Over the course of his career, he's played desert visionaries (*Lawrence of Arabia*), mercurial directors (*The Stunt Man*), genius scientists (*Creator*), and Henry II (*The Lion in Winter* and *Becket*). So Jesus doesn't seem like all that much of a stretch—though in **The Ruling Class** (1972), a black satire based on a stage play by Peter Barnes, O'Toole isn't really playing Jesus. He's playing a son of British nobility who is a paranoid schizophrenic and *thinks* he's Jesus. Such is O'Toole's greatness that he can balance the craziness and messianic fervor in equal measure. It's possible to believe that he could actually be the Son of God—or, at least, that the real Son of God had to have been a little crazy Himself.

When a respected and beloved member of the peerage, the Thirteenth Earl of Gurney (Harry Andrews), dies via misadventure during a session of autoerotic asphyxiation, Jack Gurney (O'Toole) inherits his father's wealth and position. To the dismay of the rest of the family, Jack is ill suited for the demands of English respectability, given his tendency to spout off about love and worship, and to hang from the giant cross he keeps in the living room. Sir Charles (William Mervyn) decides that the only solution is to marry Jack to Charles's mistress (Carolyn Seymour), so the mistress can produce an heir and Jack can go back to the asylum. But the social pressures of his position drive Jack's madness into a more acceptable, if far more dangerous, form...

Monty Python was never afraid of taking the piss out of those in authority, and fans will appreciate *Class*'s utterly vicious portrayal of lords and ladies as selfish, sex-obsessed, puritanical creeps. Not to give too much away, but the film's nastiest stab is the idea that Jack is unsuitable for Earldom less because he's crazy, and more because he preaches tolerance and open-minded joy. At just over two and a half hours, *Class* runs a little long, but there's enough variety—including a handful of surprise musical numbers—to hold attention throughout.

Satire is done with a purpose in mind. By exaggerating the worst qualities of a specific target, the satirist draws attention to those qualities with an aim to undermine them by making it impossible for anyone to take the original version seriously ever again. Parody is more lighthearted, and is generally done by people with a real fondness for whatever it is they're mocking. The parodist will do the same sort of exaggerations as the satirist, but without the destructive intentions. In *Flying Circus*, the Pythons were more interested in satire than parody; for the troupe, comedy was nearly always a kind of assault, even if that assault was of a largely genial sort. But their two most successful films, *Monty Python and the Holy Grail* and *Life of Brian*, were both based on genre parody: *Holy Grail* lampooned Arthurian legend (at least how it was traditionally depicted on-screen), while *Life of Brian* took aim at the risible pomposity of Biblical epics like *The Ten Commandments* and *The Robe*.

There's a reason these two movies work better than the Pythons' sketch-centric films: a storyline, even one as meandering and ridiculous as the one in *Holy Grail*, helps to hold an audience's attention, adding to the humor and covering over any of the weaker spots. It would be difficult to find a weak patch in Mel Brooks's 1974 Western spoof ***Blazing Saddles***. Brooks's third feature film would set the course for much of the rest of his career. A broad gag machine that takes the Western genre as its starting point before broadening out in seemingly every direction imaginable, *Saddles* has all the energy of a Borscht Belt comedian at his most manic, flinging punch lines and pratfalls and sight gags and dick jokes at a steady speed without regard to propriety or tact. As well, it's a movie that understands the value of good characters, with a cast that manages to be both likable and entirely ridiculous.

Cleavon Little stars as Bart, a black railroad worker who gets shanghaied into taking over the sheriff's job in the town of Rock Ridge. It's all part of the evil Hedley Lamarr's (Harvey Korman) scheme to throw the town into chaos so he can buy the land cheap and profit when the railroad comes through. The people of Rock Ridge, being by and large no sharper than the average sack of doorknobs, don't take kindly to an African American sheriff, and chaos nearly ensues just as Lamarr intended. Only Bart is smarter than the lot of them combined and sets to work saving his job, even if that means keeping a town of idiot racists from destroying themselves. In this aim, he's helped by Gene Wilder as Jim, the Waco Kid, a drunken gunfighter looking for a shot at redemption, and Madeline Kahn as Lily von Shtupp, a former associate of Lamarr's who's won over by Bart's considerable, ahem, charms.

The cast is across-the-board terrific; in addition to Little, Wilder, Kahn, and Korman working at their peak, Slim Pickens does great work as Lamarr's ill-meaning but dimwitted second in command, and Rock Ridge is populated by a gaggle of talented buffoons. *Saddles* gets a lot of mileage out of holding to no specific high or low standard for its gags. It's a movie that can make meta jokes (at one point, Bart holds himself hostage to stave off the attack of a hostile populace, and that's long before the film's fourth-wall breaking finale), use character-based humor, and not be ashamed to also make what was at that point the longest fart joke in the history of cinema. Not all of it works (which is a refrain that will come up often in discussions of parody), but it's all so cheerfully venal and good-natured that even the jokes that don't land are still entertaining.

Plus, the story and character manage to carry a lot—ridiculous as the movie is, it still takes the time to establish who everyone is, and provides a surprisingly coherent plot. This is a quality *Saddles* shares with Mel Brooks's other classic parody, **Young Franken-stein**. Released the same year as *Saddles*, *Frankenstein* takes the horror genre as its main target, aiming mostly at early Universal monster movies like *Frankenstein* and *Bride of Frankenstein*. Like *Saddles*, *Frankenstein* is as much about celebrating the clichés and tropes of the genre as it is about poking fun, pulling together another stellar cast (many of whom had worked with Brooks on *Saddles*) to tell the tale of the latest scion of the literature's first mad scientist, and his attempts to follow in his grandfather's footsteps.

Wilder takes lead point this time out as Dr. Frederick Frankenstein ("Fronk-en-steen!"), a scientist who has spent his career distancing himself from the infamy of the family name. But of course that can't last forever, because if it did, there wouldn't be much of a movie, so Frederick is called back to the family home in Transylvania. There, he meets Igor (Marty Feldman), a hunchback in denial, and the lovely Inga (Teri Garr), and, despite his best efforts, surrenders to a cinematic imperative and sets about bringing dead tissue to life. He succeeds in making a monster (Peter Boyle), but there are a few hitches in the process; considering the townsfolk, led by often incomprehensible Inspector Kemp (Kenneth Mars), are already suspicious, this may not lead to a happy ending.

Well, it does lead to a happy ending, because, as with *Saddles*, much of the charm of *Frankenstein* comes from the obvious fondness Brooks and the cast have for their characters and the world they inhabit. While the two Python satires are often bleak and cynical, Brooks's films have a boundless optimism that's matched only by their affection for cheap shots. It's a balance Brooks would struggle and fail to achieve as a director in the years following 1974, but it's hard to dispute the effectiveness of these two successes. While some of the references may have aged, the cheerful bawdiness and strong performances remain as fresh and entertaining as ever.

"Cheerful bawdiness" is a term that can well be applied to Brooks's most obvious successor in the "anything for a laugh film parody" genre, the 1980 disaster movie spoof ***Airplane!*** Jim Abrahams and David and Jerry Zucker made their film debut with 1977's *The Kentucky Fried Movie*. Directed by John Landis, *Kentucky Fried* is the film version of a selection of the trio's sketches written while they were working as an improvisational theater troupe in Wisconsin. *Airplane!* marks their first outing as a directorial team and their first big hit. While *Airplane!* follows in the footsteps of other film parodies, its zanier, more frenetic approach helped to redefine the style for decades to come.

Robert Hays stars as Ted Stryker, an ex-combat pilot and taxi driver with "a drinking problem" trying to hold on to a failing relationship with stewardess Elaine Dickinson (Julie Hagerty). In a last-ditch attempt to win her back, Stryker buys a ticket for Dickinson's next flight, little realizing that a bad batch of fish is about to put him back in the place he most fears: the cockpit. The story, taken largely from the 1957 film *Zero Hour!*, is roughly coherent. When food poisoning takes out the entire flight crew, Stryker has to face his fear of flying, as well as re-establish trust with his old commander on the ground, to land the plane safely and save everyone on board.

Like Brooks's films, the jokes come fast and furious; in fact, *Airplane!* has an even higher gag-per-minute ratio than *Saddles* or *Frankenstein*, and, while the characters are likable and clearly defined, the movie's emphasis is more on puns, sight gags, and wordplay than on relationships. Hays and Hagerty make solid heroes, and the ensemble is full of well-known dramatic actors whose serious demeanor contrasts sharply against the absurdity of their dialogue. Robert Stack and Peter Graves add a measure of gravitas to the proceedings, which is constantly undercut by the madness surrounding them, while Leslie Nielsen and Lloyd Bridges essentially redefined their onscreen personae here, as straight men trapped in a loony tunes world.

That cartoon comparison is apt for *Airplane!*, as ZAZ pushed the spoof genre even further into absurdity. While the movie nominally targets self-serious disaster films, its only real credo is "anything for a laugh," working towards a sense of anarchy that, when successful, creates enough goofy, grinning energy to make even the most obvious groaners land well. ZAZ would take this credo with them into their short-lived cop show spoof, *Police Squad!*, and when that series failed, they returned to the big screen in 1984 with ***Top Secret!***.

A parody of spy films and half a dozen other subjects, *Top* stars Val Kilmer as Nick Rivers, an American pop star who gets inadvertently dragged into the struggles of the resistance against the evil East German government and their plans to take over the world. The setting allows for gags about Nazi war movies, fifties pop music, under-pressure romance, *The Blue Lagoon*, and so many more topics it's hard to keep them all straight. Kilmer is the most readily recognizable cast member (Omar Sharif and Peter Cushing make brief cameos), demonstrating a light touch that would largely disappear in the later years of his career. *Top* wasn't anywhere near as much of a financial success as *Airplane!*, nor did it have the same cultural impact; it lacks the latter movie's frenetic pacing and the iconic recasting of stolid B-movie character actors. But it's still a funny, sweet picture.

The ZAZ parody machine wouldn't return to the genre again until 1988's ***The Naked Gun: From the Files of Police Squad!*** Movies have been based off TV shows before, but *Naked Gun* is one of the first times a failed show made its way to the big screen—although, given that the original *Police Squad!* wasn't exactly mythology-rich, familiarity with it wasn't a requirement for enjoying *Naked Gun. Gun* was officially David Zucker's solo directorial debut, but Abrahams and Jerry Zucker executive-produced as well as worked on the screenplay, and the ZAZ hallmarks are all over the film. Leslie Nielsen returns to the role of Frank Drebin, a bumbling cop with a habit of stumbling into crime and destroying city property. George Kennedy plays Frank's superior, Captain Ed Hocken, a role originated in the television series by Alan North, and O.J. Simpson takes over for Peter Lupus as the hapless Nordberg.

Gun follows Drebin's attempts to stop an evil businessman (Ricardo Montalbán) from assassinating Queen Elizabeth II via hypnosis, and the film has a clearer storyline than any episode of the television series, even throwing in a relationship for its hero with the lovely Jane Spenser (a post-Elvis Priscilla Presley). Nielsen anchors the film, taking his straight-man-slightly-skewed work from *Airplane!* and *Police Squad!* and skewing it still further into bumbling oblivion. *Gun* found success where *Squad!* couldn't, and the film led to two sequels.

If *Airplane!* set the tone for the modern spoof movie—stuffed with jokes, low- and highbrow comedy, less invested in story and character—the success of *Naked Gun* helped solidify it. Jim Abrahams had his own solo hit in the 1991 *Top Gun* style parody **Hot Shots!** The '90s marked a transition further and further into the hit-or-miss spoof movie: comedies that relied increasingly on topical references and reenactments of familiar cinematic moments over solid structure and storytelling, in a trend that would ultimately reach its nadir with cheap, tossed-off novelties like *Epic Movie* and *Date Movie*. These films were less about jokes and more about generating audience good-will through references to shared cultural moments; instantly disposable and critically reviled, the *[Blank] Movie* series turns the art of satire into flaccid regurgitation.

Spoofs work better when they have a definite target; one of the main complaints against the run of parody films that have flooded theaters in recent years is that they don't have a main focus. This is not an accusation one can make against **Wet Hot American Summer** (2001). Set at a camp in Maine at the tail end of summer 1981, the movie sets its sights on one certain genre: the summer camp comedy, like 1979's *Meatballs*. *Wet Hot* works in jokes about under-dog sports movies, sci-fi disasters, rom-coms, and rampant drug use, but the core idea remains the same, and that makes it work. With a strong structure and a great cast, this is a movie that should please any Pythonite, provided he or she hasn't been out in the sun too long.

It doesn't hurt that *Wet Hot* was created by key personnel from *The State*, one of the best TV sketch comedies of past thirty years. David Wain and Michael Showalter wrote the screenplay, and Wain directed, while Showalter stars as Gerald "Coop" Cooperberg, a nebbishy camp counselor with a crush on fellow counselor Katie (Marguerite Moreau), who, as these things tend to go, is currently dating a good-looking asshole counselor, Andy (Paul Rudd). The cast has more *State* alumni, including Ken Marino, Michael Ian Black, and Joe Lo Truglio, as well as talents like Elizabeth Banks, Amy Poehler, and Molly Shannon, and a host of others. Janeane Garofalo rules the roost as Beth, head counselor and generally nice lady, who's quietly in love with Henry Newman (David Hyde Pierce), an astrophysics professor at the local college.

Wet Hot has plenty of meta-commentary and winks at its audience, but the movie never comes across as tediously clever or simply making references for reference's sake. The setting helps—while the film is shot in Pennsylvania, not Maine, the use of an actual summer camp helps add verisimilitude to all the silliness. The cast chemistry is terrific, and Wain's direction, and his and Showalter's script, have a clear, fond understanding of the tropes they set out to satirize. Which is really what sets *Wet Hot* apart. It's as much a celebration of those silly camp movies as it is a riff on them, and its affection for its characters, however childish they may be, makes as much an escape from the tedium of day-to-day as the films it parodies. Pythonites should enjoy the work of smart people being very foolish, and the chance to laugh at a number from *Godspell*.

Edgar Wright, who made a name for himself as a writer and director on British television in the '90s and early '00s, directed his first feature film, **Shaun of the Dead**, in 2004. **Dead** takes its cues from the traditional zombie horror: an inexplicable apocalypse hits London and the world, bringing the dead back to life and driving the reanimated corpses with a hunger for human flesh. Every person a zombie bites will eventually become a zombie as well, which understandably causes problems for the movie's leading man, Shaun (Simon Pegg), an underachiever who splits his time between lowballing life with his best friend Ed (Nick Frost) and disappointing his perpetually patient girlfriend, Liz (Kate Ashfield). When Shaun lets down Liz one last time, she ends the relationship. But then the dead start rising, and Shaun has to become an unlikely hero to win back his girl and not get all his friends killed.

Dead is more linear than any of the Python films, and far more interested in character arcs and (gasp) plotting: it's less a satire than a black comedy with a surprising amount of heart. Wright's second film, **Hot Fuzz** (2007), follows in this same vein, upping the absurdity for a parody of the modern, over-the-top action film set in the small English village of Hampstead. Simon Pegg once again takes the lead, this time as Nicholas Angel, a cop so good at his job that his superiors transfer him because he's making everyone else in the department look bad. Once he arrives in Hampstead, Angel starts to find signs of a dark conspiracy of death, and he befriends the doofy son of the local police chief, Danny Butterman (Nick Frost.).

Where *Shaun* mocked zombie clichés, *Fuzz* takes on the ultra-stylized violence of Michael Bay movies, with equally entertaining results. Both movies are brilliantly cast, with plenty of faces familiar to comedy fans (Jessica Hynes, Pegg's *Spaced* costar, has a cameo in *Shaun*, and Timothy Dalton nearly steals the show in *Fuzz*). In addition to their genre targets, both movies share a decided fondness for their subject matter, as well as a satisfying, and sometimes surprisingly dramatic, compassion for their ensembles. Python's movies tend to be a little slapdash, and zany to the point of misanthropy—even *Brian*, which at least sympathizes with its lead, borders on nihilistic in its portrayal of a word full of easily led, perpetually violent morons. Wright's first two films are nearly as funny as the Pythons' best work and also manage to tell coherent, engaging stories.

Monty Python knew how to use music and knew how to use it well. Some of the troupe's best-loved bits, like "The Lumberjack Sketch" and "The Philosopher's Song," combine catchy tunes with clever lyrics to make a sketch you can sing in the shower. But while the songs are fun to listen to, no one would accuse the Pythons of musical depth. That wasn't the point—the troupe's main focus was sketch comedy, not tuneful pastiche satire. For Pythonites who wants to whistle more while they watch, writer-director Brian De Palma's 1974 movie musical **Phantom of the Paradise** may fit the bill. As '70s cult rock operas go, it's not as well known as *The Rocky Horror Picture Show* (1975), another fun, subversive treat, but *Phantom* is less interested in transgressing sexual mores, and more interested in trippy horror comedy and De Palma's signature cinematic style.

Phantom uses the classic structure of Gaston Leroux's 1910 novel *The Phantom of the Opera* as a springboard to critique an ever-hungry-for-the-next-thing music industry, one that willingly sacrifices new acts on the altar of novelty with nary a care for that act's best interests. Winslow Leach (William Finley) is a songwriter deeply committed to his art. He's working on a cantata—a cantata!—based on the story of Faust, and one night he performs a song from the cantata for Swan (Paul Williams, who also wrote the film's score), a successful record producer with at best questionable ethics. Swan decides the song is great, but the performer has to go, so he gets an underling to steal Leach's music, and then proceeds to screw Leach over as thoroughly as possible. After surviving a beating, wrongful incarceration, and getting his head crushed by a record press, Leach sneaks into Swan's new theater, the Paradise, adopts the identity of the Phantom, and works to get his revenge. Only there's more to Swan than meets the eye, and he'll use anything—including Phoenix (Jessica Harper), a young singer and object of Leach's affections—to get what he wants.

Phantom comes early in De Palma's career, when he was still experimenting with comedy and fear effects, and the movie is a great blend of the two genres. Finley, who spends most of the movie done up like a kind of sadomasochistic robot pigeon, makes for a sympathetic, if sometimes creepy, lead, and Harper is appropriately vulnerable. Gerrit Graham is great as an effeminate glam-rock heavy metal superstar. But the movie belongs to Paul Williams and De Palma. Williams's music jumps from teen-idol pop to surf songs to love ballads, and his turn as the maniacal Swan puts the diminutive performer's stature and appearance to excellent effect. His villain is a sly devil who already knows he's damned, and this is a movie that knows the best music comes out of souls just a few steps ahead of the flames.

Romantic comedies tend to tell audiences what they wish was true about relationships, rather than what actually is true. Just as action movies ignore physics and the realities of gun mechanics, a rom-com puts aside emotional complexity and practicality in favor of pop song montages and dramatic kissing. This can be done well, but the best rom-coms are more comedies-with-drama-that-also-feature-a-bit-of-romance. They show how love is as much a mixed bag as anything in this life, but that having it is still generally better than not. Of these, writer-director Woody Allen's ***Annie Hall*** (1977) may just be the best of the best: a sometimes goofy, often dry, playfully intellectual, warmly sarcastic movie about two people who aren't quite perfect enough for each other.

Woody Allen stars as Alvy Singer, a Woody Allen–type stand-up who spends his days worrying about the eventual heat death of the universe, and his nights trying to get laid. One day he meets Annie Hall (Diane Keaton), a charmingly scattered sweetheart. The two start dating, fall for each other hard, and work through the ups and downs of coupledom in the 1970s. Alvy tries to further his career as a stand-up while resisting the lowered standards represented by his lecherous best friend (Tony Roberts), while Annie takes college courses, opens her mind, and considers starting a singing career at the behest of a quietly sleazy Hollywood type (the wonderfully cast-against-type Paul Simon).

As far as plot goes, that's basically it. Allen's original script for *Hall* was focused on a murder mystery that failed to make it into the final cut; instead, the released film is a collection of sketches and musings on dating and New York and the irritations of semi-fame, tied together by Alvy and Annie's relationship. Diane Keaton does some of her best work here as a charming scatterbrain more than equal to Allen, and the cast as a whole (including a cameo by a young Christopher Walken) is terrific. Pythonites will appreciate the movie's fourth-wall breaking and general cleverness. Everyone will appreciate a movie that tells you that even "meant to be" may not be "meant forever"—and that's okay, in the end.

Peter Sellers's final film, *The Fiendish Plot of Dr. Fu Manchu* (1980), isn't all that great; it's certainly not the kind of swan song the actor deserved. For that, Sellers fans and Pythonites would do better to turn to Sellers's second-to-last film, **Being There** (1979), a gentle, biting social satire about an idiot savant who finds himself influencing some of the most powerful men in the world. The role of Chance the Gardener, a cipher whose greatest gift is his ability to reflect back to people whatever it is they want to see, seems tailor-made for Sellers, who made a living putting on other faces without ever showing much of his own. *Being There* isn't as outright farcical as Sellers's best-known film roles, and the actor doesn't do multiple characters for once, but the movie is just as important to understanding his legacy as any other.

When his wealthy employer dies, Chance is left without a place in the world. The mansion where he spent his life tending to the garden gets closed up, and he's forced to go out into the streets without any idea what adult life is actually like, apart from what he's seen on television. His fortunes change for the better when Eve Rand (Shirley MacLaine) hits him with her husband's car. Eve is married to Ben Rand (Melvyn Douglas), a rich businessman with some powerful friends, and when Eve brings Chance home to tend his (minor) injuries, her husband is impressed by the former gardener's bland niceties about tending plants. This leads to Ben introducing Chance to the President of the United Stated (Jack Warden), and soon Chance is being heralded as a visionary, despite a naivety so profound it's nearly angelic.

Being There only really has one joke—why doesn't anyone recognize the idiot's platitudes, which wouldn't be out of place in a garden-themed fortune cookie, for what they are? But it plays that joke to the hilt, eschewing obvious gags in favor of sweetly understated slow burn. Director Hal Ashby, working off a script by Robert C. Jones and Jerzy Kosinski (who wrote the novel *Being There* is based on), puts the audience in the position of rooting for Chance to succeed, regardless of what that success may say about the insight of America's great thinkers. In this, he's helped ably by Sellers, who disappears into a man who, at times, doesn't really seem to exist at all. Sellers captures the sense of mirrored surfaces without ever winking or drawing attention to Chance's empty-headed prophecy. The result is a haunting, deeply goofy, humanely cynical story about a world much like our own, where the only wisdom we're willing to hear is the stuff we think we already know.

Albert Brooks's first movie is entirely of its time—and, lucky for us, that that time just happens to be today. While **Real Life** was released in 1979, its premise is so familiar to modern audiences that it's nearly mundane: Albert Brooks, playing a filmmaker named Albert Brooks, decides to film a real family for a year in hopes of professional acclaim and financial reward. These days, reality programming is a routine fact of life, as television schedules are filled with shows that purport to present normal people squaring off against each other in unscripted drama. The question has always been how much of that conflict is created by the shows' producers, and that's the question at the heart of *Real Life*, so that even if the concept isn't as fresh as it once was, its concerns remain relevant.

Actually, one of the central (and best) jokes of *Real Life* is that the question of outsider interference is answered almost immediately. Brooks chooses the Yeager family, a white, middle-class clan from Phoenix, Arizona, to be the focus of his experiment (the other finalist family for the film is rejected because of Wisconsin winters). He installs himself in a house across the street from the Yeagers' home, filming them with special helmet cameras, and keeps a team of psychologists and experts on hand at all times to assess how the Yeagers handle the stress and complications of being constantly observed. Things go wrong almost immediately, because Brooks is no impartial observer; his ego and narcissism drive him to interfere with his test subjects in all sorts of unfortunate ways.

As the head of the Yeager family, Charles Grodin handles his perpetual humiliation with a calm that doesn't quite cover the despair, and as his wife, Frances Lee McCain manages to convey ennui and frustration without overstating either. Really, though, Brooks is the star here, and the point of *Real Life* becomes clear very quickly: however much the director claims to be interested in showing his subjects "as they are," his primary concern is in telling the story he wants to tell, whatever the consequences. In Brooks's case, that story is one of high drama and award-winning insight, and the lengths he'll go to in order to achieve this generate the movie's biggest laughs.

Steve Martin made his debut as a leading man in **The Jerk**, director Carl Reiner's 1979 comedy about a man who stumbles onto success and, well, everything else. Martin had already proven himself a comedy superstar, a stand-up capable of filling stadiums with adoring fans, and while he'd cameoed in films before (including a memorable appearance in *The Muppet Movie*), *The Jerk* was Martin's first chance to bring his own particular brand of comic philosophy to the screen. The story of Navin Johnson, Martin's goony alter ego, is a rags-to-riches-to-rags odyssey that perfectly encapsulates the "so stupid it's brilliant" aesthetic. The gags in *The Jerk* are broader than some very broad thing, possibly the side of a barn, but that's part of the humor.

It's a style familiar to Python fans. One of the troupe's recurring sketches featured a broad idiot caricature, called a Gumby, generally used to break up longer sketches; Navin is essentially a Gumby with slightly more character depth. That character depth is what makes the movie work. Nobody would ever mistake Martin's performance here as the high point of his acting career (although it is excellent), but by giving his Gumby a sweet soul and just a slight hint of sadness, he turns a one-joke bit into something that can sustain a whole hour and a half without getting old. Python's anarchic sensibility rarely had much compassion for the fools caught in its wake, but while many of *The Jerk*'s best jokes are at Navin's expense, there's never any real threat of mayhem or darkness here. This may turn some fans off, but they'd be missing out on a genial, terrific film. Martin's later comedies are increasingly hit or miss (marred by a sense of commercial calculation that neatly excises any possibility of self-awareness), but for a while, he was as bold, innovative, and crazy as the Pythons at their best.

Equally as outrageous as *The Jerk*, and far riskier, was Reiner and Martin's next film together, **Dead Men Don't Wear Plaid** (1982). Working off a script by Reiner, Martin, and George Gipe, *Dead Men* eschews traditional filming techniques to tell a classic film noir mystery with just a little twist. Martin stars as Rigby Reardon, a private dick with a taste for the ladies, who gets in over his head when he agrees to look into the murder of Juliet Forrest's (Rachel Ward) dead father. *Dead Men* uses clips from older movies like *The Big Sleep* and *The Bribe*, inserting Martin into scenes so he can land jokes opposite Humphrey Bogart, Barbara Stanwyck, Vincent Price, and others. It's an odd notion for a full-length movie, and part of the fun is trying to identify where each clip came from before the end credits, as well as seeing just how long the filmmakers can sustain such a patchwork narrative. But if *Dead Men* is an oddity, it's still a fun one, and Martin does surprisingly well at keeping pace with long-gone stars.

Reiner and Martin's third movie, **The Man With Two Brains** (1983), was a return to the more traditional wackiness of *The Jerk*. In this parody of science fiction films like *The Brain That Wouldn't Die* (1962), Martin plays Dr. Michael Hfuhruhurr, a brilliant neurosurgeon who's unlucky in love. Hfuhruhurr accidentally runs over the beautiful Dolores Benedict (Kathleen Turner) with his car and marries her, little realizing that she's a gold-digging shrew out to kill him and steal his fortune. But then sometimes love comes in ways you don't expect. When the good doctor (you try typing "Hfuhruhurr" out more than twice) pays a visit to a mad scientist colleague (David Warner), he makes a psychic connection with a brain in a jar voiced by an uncredited Sissy Spacek. The two are soon completely smitten with each other, but the brain's lack of a body raises certain difficulties for long-term relationships. It's up to our hero to find a solution before his new love fades away forever in this goofy, goony motion picture.

Martin actually worked with Python in their 1989 special *Parrot Sketch Not Included—20 Years of Monty Python*, a collection of sketches from *Flying Circus* that Martin introduced and hosted. But the comedian never really collaborated with the troupe on a project, which is a shame. **Dirty Rotten Scoundrels** (1988), a Frank Oz film in which Martin costars with Michael Caine, is about as close as the world ever got to such a collaboration, pitting the sophistication and wit of the cultured English against the smarmy lewdness of America. Actually, that's a bit of stretch—Python was as lewd as anybody. But the fact is, *Scoundrels* is a terrific movie no matter how you look at it.

A remake of the 1964 film *Bedtime Story* with David Niven and Marlon Brando, *Scoundrels* stars Caine and Martin as a pair of con men with very difference styles. Caine seduces older women with the promise of adventure and romance; Martin goes for the short con, begging food money based on stories about an ailing grandmother. The two attempt to team up, but their disparate approaches create tension, and they end up squaring off against each other, battling for the wealth and affection of the hapless Glenne Headly. *Scoundrels* gives Martin a chance to act *and* do some great slapstick, and his and Caine's chemistry together is strong throughout.

Throughout Monty Python's *Monty Python and the Holy Grail*, the film will intermittently cut away from the main action to show action in the "modern" world. The first cut is to a historian lecturing on the legend of King Arthur (the film's supposed leading man), before a knight rides across and cuts his throat. From then on, a handful of cutaways show a police homicide investigation in process, and the movie ends with officers interrupting Arthur's attempt to storm the castle where the French are holding the Grail. It's not the best climax the troupe ever devised, but it fits their obsession with constantly drawing attention to the conventions of filming. It's an obsession that ran throughout their career, a way of commenting on jokes as they happened that made watching *Flying Circus* an exhilarating, if occasionally unnerving, experience.

The same could be said for Richard Rush's 1980 cult classic, **The Stunt Man**. Steve Railsback stars as Cameron, a Vietnam vet on the run from the police who stumbles onto a movie set in the middle of filming. Cameron inadvertently causes the death of a stunt man by interfering with a stunt, but director Eli Cross (Peter O'Toole) is intrigued enough by Cameron's shaky charisma that he invites the vet to take the dead man's place. This means a hideout from the cops, a higher paycheck than vagrancy has to offer, and the possibility of romancing the movie's leading lady, Nina Franklin (Barbara Hershey). But the life of a stunt man is a dangerous one, and, given his experiences in the war and his rough treatment at the hands of the police, Cameron isn't one to trust easily. The question becomes, is Eli trying to kill him? And if he isn't, just what's going on here?

The Stunt Man is an intoxicating mixture of dark comedy, action, romance, and satire, and mere plot summary can't hope to capture the film's constantly shifting tone. Scenes from the movie-within-a-movie cut into regular scenes with their own peculiar rhythm, and O'Toole rules over everything in one of his best roles, a director who thinks he's God and just might be right. *Stunt* isn't as overwhelmingly riotous as Python at its best, but the movie shares the troupe's willingness to poke holes in anything in sight, including the scenery, just to see what happens next. It's a style that's tough to manage (poke too many holes and there's nothing left *but* holes, which isn't funny, just sad), but Python largely managed it, and so does Rush here.

One of Monty Python's great strengths is its ability to transcend culture; it's perfectly possible to be a firm fan of the troupe if you're British or American or Chinese or perhaps some form of Martian gifted with the ability to perceive the same visual spectrum as humans. ("Holy Glicknar," you'd most likely say in such a case, communicated to the life-mate currently gnawing its way through your dorsal stomach, "That 'Confuse-a-Cat' sketch is the smarzmazziest!" And then your mate would finish the sexual act of digesting your external organs, and the two of you would spend a pleasant evening together as your life-mate buried your secondary corpse.) But it can be difficult, as a foreigner, to understand some of *Flying Circus*'s more topical references. The Pythons would often satirize BBC convention, and while the results were entertaining regardless of their original context, there's still a little bit of confusion for anyone who isn't familiar with the joke's target. Sometimes watching *Flying Circus* (which is generally more directly satirical than the films) can be, for the outsider, like landing in a foreign land where things are almost, but not quite, exactly the same.

For those, we offer *An American Werewolf in London*, Jon Landis's 1981 horror comedy about, well, you read the title, right? David Naughton stars as a college student traveling abroad with his friend Griffin Dunne. One night while walking on the moors under a full moon, the two make the mistake of disobeying the locals' injunctions and wander off the path, where they fall pray to a large, vicious wolf. Dunne is killed, but Naughton wakes up in London hospital, where he flirts with pretty nurse Jenny Agutter and mourns his friend. Only Dunne isn't resting easy. The ghost (who looks less like a ghost and more like a rotting corpse) appears to Naughton to warn him that he's been infected by a werewolf, and that he's doomed to transform into a horrible monster at the next full moon.

American Werewolf works well as a horror movie, full of sympathetic characters and great scare scenes, but it's also a surprisingly funny dark comedy. Dunne's wisecracking apparition never grows stale (even as his body does), but more relevant to the topic at hand is the ongoing culture clash between the increasingly panicky American and the London he finds full of stiff-upper-lippers and balloon-wielding children. Anyone who has ever sat through an episode of *Flying Circus* wondering just who the hell the news presenters are supposed to be poking fun at will find some sympathy here as Naughton struggles to understand British television, British etiquette, and his own tortured soul.

Speaking of strangers in strange lands, it would be hard to picture someone more out of place than Jeff Goldblum in *The Tall Guy* (1989). Performing on stage as the silent straight man to the overwrought gesticulations of main attraction Rowan Atkinson, Goldblum is a miserable, sneezing mess. He sticks out in a crowd and wanders at bent angles through a London full of misfits and oddities, an American abroad lost in a sea of quirkiness. His personal life is even worse than his professional life, until one day, while visiting the hospital for his standard round of ineffective allergy shots, he meets a nurse played by Emma Thompson. Thompson's beauty and dry wit knock him head over heels, and he immediately sets to wooing her. But as their relationship thrives, his exuberance can't help but shine through in his theatrical work—upstaging Atkinson, who immediately cans him. What's a tall, out-of-work actor to do?

The Tall Guy is Richard Curtis's first film script. Curtis, best known these days for penning charming but light romantic comedies like *Bridget Jones's Diary* and *Love Actually*, started his career with the far more biting *Black Adder* series (see Chapter 4). *Tall Guy*, which was produced between the third and fourth *Black Adder* series, serves as something of a bridge between the darker work of Curtis's early period and the more populist rom-coms to come. *Tall Guy* is never precisely dark, but Rowan Atkinson plays a largely irredeemable bastard, a self-absorbed egoist who can't handle even the slightest threat of competition; and Goldblum's follow-up job, as the leading man in a musical version of *The Elephant Man*, is a good-natured but still sharp satire of theater at its most ridiculously self-important.

On the other hand, Goldblum's relationship with Thompson is as sweet and charming as anything in Curtis's career. If *The Tall Guy* has a fault, it's that it's a little *too* light; the movie clocks in at just under an hour and a half, and the script doesn't feel completely realized. Atkinson, the film's antagonist, is only in a handful of scenes, and the third-act complication that threatens to break the leads apart is poorly motivated and resolves too easily. Still, the lack of drama may be an asset for some, and the brisk pace makes *The Tall Guy* a perfect lazy Sunday diversion. Goldblum and Thompson (in her film debut) have great chemistry, and Python fans will enjoy the scenes from *Elephant!* as well as Atkinson at his smarmy, slimy best.

While punk as a genre didn't make its official debut until some time in the mid '70s, the art of being artless wasn't an entirely new idea. In a sense, the greatest comedy has always had a certain sneer and swagger to it, given that it so often works to poke holes in pretensions and mock the so-called unmockable. Monty Python spent much of its career snickering at the sophisticate and the fool alike. The show's willingness to walk off mid-joke, to change direction whenever the writers got bored, is very punk, and it's possible to draw a line between the more anarchic, freewheeling shows and films that came in later decades, like for instance **Repo Man**, a thoroughly American punk movie made in 1984 by British director Alex Cox. *Repo Man* has the Python knack for surrealism as well as a touch of the show's cheery nihilism.

A never-better Emilio Estevez stars as Otto Madox, an aimless Los Angeles delinquent who gets inadvertently sucked into the low-stakes, high-contempt world of automobile repossession. As his mentor, Bud, Harry Dean Stanton teaches him the rules and ropes of the trade, and Otto takes to it with surprising ease, not caring so much about screwing over the poor, but just happy to have something to do. As he hones his skills of lying and occasionally getting beaten up, a desperate stranger rolls into town, driving a car with something so horrible in the trunk that it can instantly vaporize anyone who sees it.

These two stories do eventually connect, as Bud becomes determined to track down the stranger's vehicle and collect the substantial reward, but really, *Repo Man* is a thrill not so much for its tight plotting as for its richly textured world. The ensemble here covers a wide variety of mental illnesses, but each character is well developed, and background details reward the attentive viewer, like the grocery store items with the white labels reading "Food," or the way Bud's Repo Code sounds suspiciously like science fiction writer Isaac Asimov's Laws of Robotics. What it all adds up to is open to debate, but this is a silly movie made for smart people, and it's hard to get more Pythonesque than that.

It's no simple task to judge just how important **This Is Spinal Tap** (1984) is to modern comedy. Rob Reiner's movie about an over-the-hill British heavy metal band struggling to remain relevant in a relentlessly indifferent world helped to popularize the concept of the "mockumentary"—a fictional film shot like a documentary that uses its intimacy with its subjects to create ironic juxtapositions between their self-image and "reality." Which is just a fancy way of saying *Spinal Tap* is part of the train that led to the original *Office*, which in turn helped define the sitcom style that dominates today's television landscape.

Really, the important fact to take away here is that *Spinal Tap* is brutally, brilliantly hilarious. Michael McKean, Christopher Guest, and Harry Shearer star as the lead members of the titular group. The movie follows them through a disastrous tour of the United States, where the clueless trio (along with their manager, keyboardist, and disposable drummer) encounters hostile audiences, indifferent record company executives, and the problems caused by their own empty-headed arrogance. The largely improvised script gives the conversations a loose, casual feel, a far cry from the intricate Python writing style, but that looseness fits in perfectly with the faux-doc approach. Both the movie and the troupe share an interest in drawing attention to the absurd, and Reiner's choice of structure is somewhat akin to the Pythons' obsession with breaking the fourth wall. Really, though, Python fans will mostly just appreciate *This Is Spinal Tap* because it is a damn funny movie, and essential viewing for any fan of the form.

This Is Spinal Tap demonstrated Christopher Guest's knack for improvised satire, but it'd be another twelve years before Guest would return to the mockumentary format, with 1996's **Waiting for Guffman**. Guest's second movie as director (his first was the 1989 Hollywood satire *The Big Picture*, staring Kevin Bacon) set the model that he would follow for the next decade and a half: a group of talented comedic performers and actors, working with strong characters and a loose script, focus on a specific group of human oddities in a fictitious documentary format, a.k.a. the "mockumentary." By now, it's a form that's taken over half the television dial, as well as dozens of movies, but in *Guffman*, it still seems relatively fresh.

The small (fictional) town of Blaine, Missouri is coming up on its 150-year anniversary, and as part of the celebration, they've hired Corky St. Clair (Christopher Guest) to produce, write, and direct a show celebrating the town's history. Corky pulls together as talented a group of community theater enthusiasts as he can from the town's population, including Parker Posey, Catherine O'Hara,

Fred Willard, and Eugene Levy. With Bob Balaban as the show's harried musical director, Corky creates an awkward blend of camp, hokey sentiment, and surrealism, all while struggling with the entirely rational town government's budgetary concerns and shifting cast woes. As opening night draws near, Corky keeps hopes alive with the promise of a visit from famed theatrical critic Mort Guffman, who could be the ensemble's ticket to Broadway fame.

Guffman makes great use of the contrast between its characters' oversized ambition and the reality of their circumstances, but for such an effective parody of small-town delusion, the movie never comes across as mean-spirited or contemptuous. The songs are catchy, awful, and hilarious, and the cast manages to make their roles as likable as they are laughable. Much as *Spinal Tap* succeeded off the doofy charm of its titular band, *Guffman* works because, in its own silly way, it's as much a celebration of its leads' ridiculous ambition as it is a parody. They're idiots, but at least they care.

Director Stephen Soderbergh is best known for his biggest hits, like the Academy Award–winning *Traffic* (2000), a crime thriller about drugs with Michael Douglas and Benicio Del Toro; *Erin Brockovich* (2000), a legal drama based on a true story about a woman fighting corporate corruption, starring Julia Roberts in the title role; and the *Ocean's Eleven* series (2001, 2004, 2007), a trilogy of breezy caper films, with George Clooney and Brad Pitt running a star-studded cast of con-men and crooks. But while all these movies are worthwhile in their own way, Pythonites may find more of interest in Soderbergh's less popular, more challenging films. The director hasn't done much in the way of comedy, but his willingness to experiment, combined with a strong sense of the ridiculous, makes those comedies he has done worth a look.

In 1996, Soderbergh wrote, directed, filmed, and starred in **Schizopolis**, a very odd movie indeed. *Schizopolis* unfolds in a series of three segments, and it tells the story (sort of) of a man (Soderbergh) in a troubled marriage, working at a job that doesn't fulfill him. That job is the movie's most striking satirical hit—Soderbergh's character, Fletcher Munson, is an office drone serving under Theodore Azimuth Schwitters, an L. Ron Hubbard-like visionary in charge of a Scientology-esque cult called Eventualism. *Schizopolis* doesn't have a linear plot, and it's not exactly an outright comedy, but there are enough jokes here to make it comedy-ish, like the conversations between Munson and his wife that consist entirely of statements describing their banal exchanges, like "Generic greeting," and "Generic greeting returned."

Still, *Schizopolis* is uneven, more the work of a director trying to rediscover his voice than a classic in its own right. For the Pythonite interested in the best expression of the comedic stylings of Soderbergh, ***The Informant!*** (2009) is the way to go. Based on a true story, *The Informant!* stars Matt Damon as Mark Whitacre, an up-and-coming young executive at Archer Daniels Midland, a giant in the food-processing industry. In 1992, Whitacre confessed to the FBI that ADM had been involved with price-fixing; for years, the corporation would hold meetings with their competitors to set the market price for lysine, a chemical used on commercial livestock. Price-fixing is highly illegal, and over the next few years, Whitacre would provide tapes, documents, and testimony to the FBI about ADM's involvement in the scam. But then the FBI agents assigned to the case started noticing certain discrepancies, and they started asking questions, and things got complicated.

It doesn't sound like the starting point of a great comedy, but Soderbergh works to contrast Mark's crazed internal monologue (provided in narration by Damon) against the world with which it has no apparent connection. The film is a wash of dull browns and yellows, the boring vistas and wide-open land serving to contradict Whitacre's view of himself as a mastermind embarked on a great adventure. But while the joke is in many ways on him, *Informant!* never becomes mean-spirited or snide, instead getting laughs from the strangeness of the situation (which, again, is largely true to real-life events), and its lead's offbeat presence. Damon has rarely been better than he is here, with a performance that is at once bull-headed, chipper, and oddly vulnerable. Less of a dark comedy than a gray one, *The Informant!* is one of a kind.

· · ·

He looks like a man who died three days ago, but no one had the heart to tell him. Set in London in 1969, writer-director Bruce Robinson's **Withnail and I** (1986) is not a horror film, but as the titular Withnail, Richard E. Grant is horror enough, a thin rail of a human being, pale, sneering, cursing, and downing alcohol like it was air. Paul McGann stars as "I," Withnail's roommate and the film's nominal hero, a perpetually nervous young man who endures his friendship with Withnail like most people endure a cancer diagnosis. The two out-of-work actors live in squalor, scramble for jobs, and tear at each other constantly. Then, one day, they decide to take a vacation out in the country, and things get considerably worse. It's a comedy with yellowed, slanting teeth.

Withnail is primarily a movie of mood. The plot, such as it is, barely qualifies as farce. The two main characters leave London to spend a holiday in a cottage owned by Withnail's gregarious, homosexual Uncle Monty (Richard Griffiths). But while the setting is beautiful, the locals and the weather are not, and both men soon find themselves struggling to find food and heat. Eventually Monty himself arrives, with all the comfort money can provide, but as Withnail told his uncle that his traveling companion was gay in order to procure the cottage, circumstances quickly become even more stressful for the suffering hero. There are funny lines (most of them coming from Withnail), but much of the humor comes from the delivery, and the setting, and the general impression that everything is just about to fall apart, any minute now.

It's a vibe the film shares with much of Monty Python's work, and it balances against the real misery at the story's heart without detracting from it or wallowing in it. The hero's constant terror— of physical violence, of his own sexuality, and of how he'll manage to survive till morning—is played both for laughs and with deep sympathy. And as Withnail, Grant is a marvel of unchecked anarchy, drinking lighter fluid just to prove he can, and shouting whenever a whisper would be more appropriate. *Withnail and I* doesn't celebrate his manic behavior—the film is largely about McGann's character gradually realizing that he has to move on in a way that means living his friend behind—but it recognizes the appeal: in the face of a mediocre world, self-destruction is an awfully seductive response.

Joel and Ethan Coen made their cinematic debut with the 1984 noir-thriller *Blood Simple*, a great, quirky suspense drama about a cheating wife, a jealous husband, and one bastard of a private detective. It's a good first film, but Pythonites will find especial interest in the brothers' second film, **Raising Arizona** (1987), a comedy about couples without children, parents with too many children, and a bounty hunter from hell. While *Blood Simple* had hints of the Coens' distinct directorial perspective, with startling shots and a perverse sense of humor at the macabre proceedings, *Arizona* was almost a statement of intent.

Nicolas Cage (in one of his greatest roles) stars as H.I. McDunnough, a good-natured stooge with an addiction to robbing convenience stores. Over the course of his many incarcerations, H.I. meets and falls in love with a policewoman named Edwina (Holly Hunter), and the two marry, with H.I. swearing to go straight in the name of stable matrimony. This gets complicated when the couple learns that Edwina is incapable of bearing children. The furniture magnate Nathan Arizona, Sr. (Trey Wilson) is then blessed with the birth of quintuplets, and Edwina and H.I. decide to kidnap one of the babies to raise as their own. The situation becomes increasingly complicated from there.

The loopy story of *Arizona* is striking enough on its own, but the Coens populate the film with a world of quirky misfits whose quirks are never overly labored. It's a light film, for all its baby-napping and occasional violence, but one with a soul, in which characters' dreams are treated with the utmost seriousness, even when their methods of achieving those dreams backfire spectacularly. The line between drama and comedy is often very fine with the Coens, and nowhere is that more clear than in their 1991 film **Barton Fink.**

Fink is nearly impossible to classify. A sort of horror-comedy-thriller-drama-satire, the movie stars John Turturro as the titular playwright, a New York intellectual who comes to Hollywood after proving his genius to the theater set back home. The film industry isn't quite as he expects it, with the studio boss (Michael Lerner) assigning him to create that "Barton Fink feeling" in the confines of a traditional wrestling picture, a genre Fink knows next to nothing about. As well, the Hotel Earle, where Barton takes up residence during his stay, is an echoing, eerie building where the wallpaper peels overnight and flies feast on the unconscious. Luckily, Fink makes a friend in Charlie Meadows (John Goodman, in his greatest film role), his down-the-hall neighbor, a cheerful insurance salesman who tries to give the writer advice on the common man. Then things get worse.

Telling any more about the film would be to spoil the surprises, but safe to say, *Barton* is a glorious oddity, jumping from genre to genre without ever changing its tone. Monty Python rarely got as grim as this film gets, but they share with *Barton* (as well as with the Coens' oeuvre in general) a passion for confounding audience expectations. *Barton* may be the darkest of the Coens' comedy films, and while it has more than its share of laughs, as the story proceeds and the situation becomes increasingly dire, that laughter grows more and more desperate: the sound of a man falling down a hole, hoping that someone above might hear him and respond.

The Hudsucker Proxy (1994), the Coens' next film after *Barton* and their tribute to the '30s screwball comedy, is considerably less dire. It's also not quite as successful as their best work and sometimes fumbles its tone, but there's still plenty to like here. Tim Robbins does his usual solid work as a mail-room clerk who dreams of hitting the big time—and does—and Jennifer Jason Leigh's performance as a fast-talking reporter with a slightly tarnished heart of gold gets points for commitment. Paul Newman's terrific turn as a Machiavellian businessman undone by the powers of good helps hold the film together, and there are enough odd touches that the somewhat prosaic "innocent gets corrupted, only to be saved by the power of his innate decency and an angel who can stop time" plot never really seems all that prosaic.

More successful was the brothers' 1998 **The Big Lebowski,** starring Jeff Bridges, the story of a pothead bowler hippie who gets sucked into a web of Chandlerian intrigue when a millionaire asks his help in recovering a missing wife. A shaggy-dog plot masquerading as a mystery, *Lebowski* rambles its way through kidnappings and toe-cuttings with a tone set by its perpetually bemused protagonist, a long-suffering, genial stoner with no more ambition in life than to keep everything roughly as it is. John Goodman turns in another standout performance as Bridges' militant, paranoid best friend and bowling partner, and the movie finds much of its appeal in simply letting the two disparate personalities bounce off each other. More than any other of the Coens' films, *Lebowski* has a devoted cult following, full of fans committed to living their life in the model of Bridges' anti-detective, but the film is a delight even for non-enthusiasts: oddball, rambling, and perpetually half-baked.

The follow-up to *Lebowski*, **O Brother, Where Art Thou?** (2000), keeps with that affable tone, with a loose (very, very loose) retelling of Homer's *The Odyssey* set in 1930s Mississippi. George Clooney stars as Ulysses Everett McGill, a con on the run trying to win back his wife and daughters and stay two steps ahead of the law. He's aided in his journey by Tim Blake Nelson and John Turturro, and the trio travels the South of the Great Depression, reenacting various memorable scenes from Homer's ancient poem in a more modern context. The Coens' choice to use folk music as the film's backdrop and an occasional centerpiece holds together the often shambling plot, and while *Brother* doesn't quite hit the heights of the Coens' greatest work, it holds up as generally delightful.

Perhaps the Coens' most Pythonesque film to date is their 2008 satirical thriller, **Burn After Reading,** about a group of idiots who ruin each other's lives when they try to take themselves seriously. When ex-CIA operative Osbourne Cox (John Malkovich) decides to write an angry memoir in response to losing his job, he expects big things, but what he doesn't expect is that this memoir will fall into the hands of two gym employees (Frances McDormand and Brad Pitt) who assume the self-indulgent writing and bank information (provided by Cox's wife, who plans to divorce him) are pieces of a hugely important intelligence puzzle. The gym employees decide to blackmail Cox with the information, creating an explosion of chaos that threatens to derail their lives and the lives of everyone around them.

Burn is of particular interest to Python fans because it is full of stupid people doing stupid things, with horrible consequences. What could've been a grim, nihilistic slog is instead a fast-paced lark, and some of the wild spirit that informs the best of *Flying Circus* is clearly at play here. Really, nearly all of the Coens' films are worth a look, comedy or otherwise (although *The Ladykillers*, their 2004 remake of the Ealing Studios' film, is pretty dire, apart from a stellar performance by Tom Hanks in the Alec Guinness role), because the directors' unique perspective and idiosyncratic style is one of the most consistently engaging in all of modern cinema. Pythonites will appreciate the Coens' intelligence, wit, and timing, and their ability to be utterly ridiculous in the face of a world gone seriously mad.

Generalization is the scourge of all writers, but to say that the majority of modern fans of Monty Python weren't the coolest kids in school would not be to take a rhetorical risk. Appreciation of *Flying Circus* and the rest requires a certain knack for discernment, and in public schooling, the smarter you are, the harder the time you'll have surviving. But really, no one has it all that easy as a teenager, which is one of the reasons **Heathers** (1988) is so enduring. A dark satire about the lengths to which a person will go to fit in, and the depths to which she'll sink to get out, it's got something anyone who was ever young can relate to: the understanding that being a teenager often means wanting everyone, including yourself, dead.

In the role that would solidify her as a crush target for a generation of emotional young males, Winona Ryder stars as Veronica, a normal enough girl who's close enough to popularity to be on friendly terms with the three Heathers, Kim Walker, Lisanne Falk, and Shannen Doherty. The Heathers rule school with an iron fist, but when Veronica starts hanging out with a new student named J.D. (Christian Slater), things start to change. Especially when Veronica and J.D. "accidentally" murder the Heather in charge with a cup of drain cleaner.

The body count rises from there. *Heathers* these days is remembered mostly for its black comedy, mining laughs out of the way a vapid faculty and flaky student body respond to tragedy, and for its quality one-liners. ("Fuck me gently with a chainsaw" will never go out of style.) But the film has a certain amount of empathy for all the freaks, geeks, dweebs, jocks, drama queens, and spoiled princesses just trying to get by. High school is bad, the real world is worse, so maybe the best we can hope for is that everyone might be just a little bit nicer to each other.

To be absolutely honest, the best place to see Tom Stoppard's Shakespearean meta-comedy ***Rosencrantz and Guildenstern Are Dead*** (1990) is on the stage. That's the venue it was written for, and that's really the place most suited for a three-act meditation on the role of two minor characters in one of the greatest theatrical tragedies ever composed. But not everyone has access to live theater these days, and most regional companies are reluctant to allow audience members to dictate their schedules. Which means the only real recourse for the curious is to read the script itself—which is excellent, and a great way to catch all of Stoppard's tricks and games—or to watch the movie version, directed by Stoppard. While reading is fun, there's still a lot of pleasure in seeing the words spoken aloud by people who are paid large amounts of money largely for their ability to speak words in a convincing and entertaining fashion.

Python fans will find a lot to love here: wordplay, puns, and a commitment to the absurd, combined with strong characters and an accessible discussion of existential despair. Rosencrantz (Gary Oldman) and Guildenstern (Tim Roth) are called to Denmark to help the royal family unravel some tricky and emotionally fraught family politics. The plot will be familiar to anyone who knows anything about *Hamlet*: uncle kills king, usurps throne, marries queen, prince gets upset. But this is the background noise of *R&G*, a distant thunderhead that occasionally bursts into the main narrative just long enough to convince the two hapless heroes that *something* is going on, even if they are never quite sure what. Richard Dreyfuss costars as the Player, the leader of an acting troupe who always knows just a bit more than he's willing to let on. It all ends in tragedy, but hilariously so, and while the movie isn't quite as well-paced as it might be, it's still a solid record of one of the greatest playful plays of the twentieth century.

Sketch comedy often lives and dies on the strength of premise. Get a strong enough hook, like, say, a government agency devoted to the promotion and financing of absurd ambulations, and the battle for audience attention is halfway won. By that metric, **_Groundhog Day_** (1993), Harold Ramis's meta-physical comedy, is a sketch comedy writer's dream. Bill Murray stars as Phil Connors, an arrogant weatherman who spends his time snidely reminding everyone how much better he is than they are. On a fateful February 2, Phil travels with cameraman Larry (Chris Elliott) and cheery producer Rita (Andie MacDowell) to the small town of Punxsutawney, Pennsylvania, for their annual Groundhog Day festivities. The festivities go off without a hitch, but the trio is trapped in town by a sudden storm.

When Phil wakes up the next morning, it's the same morning as before: February 2. And it continues being February 2 for months and years beyond that. For no explicit reason, Phil is trapped in a time loop that only he's aware of, doomed to repeat the same twenty-four-hour period seemingly endlessly. It's a concept that lends itself to a host of obvious gags. Being able to predict people's behavior down to the second means finished sentences, mind-reading tricks, and well-timed physical gags. All of which _Groundhog Day_ delivers, while Phil tries to make himself a better man and win Rita's affection.

Well, eventually he gets around to doing that. What makes _Groundhog Day_ such a tremendous movie, and worthwhile viewing for Pythonites, is that it doesn't just settle for easy jokes. In one of the strongest performances of his career, Bill Murray takes Phil from callow cynicism to giddy egotism to suicidal despair to—well, to tell any more would be spoiling the fun. The movie doesn't simply provide a concept and shallowly skim the surface. It explores the ramifications of an eternity spent on a single day in a way that's accessible, entertaining, and deeply soulful. A Monty Python take on the same material might hit a few of the same gags, but this is a movie that could've coasted for ninety minutes, but instead gets as much out of its story as Phil gets out of the world's most useless holiday.

For a certain kind of American teen, growing up too smart and too bad at sports to find popularity through the usual routes in high school, Monty Python was a lifeline, a group of role models as well as a form of personal style. Adolescent Python fans in the States could quote lines and cling to obscure references as a way of defining themselves, proving their intellectual superiority and taste with lines like "Ni! Ni! Ni!" and "Nobody expects the Spanish Inquisition." It's a certain sort of nerdiness, and, while Wes Anderson's 1998 movie **Rushmore** doesn't lean on Python references, it functions as a love letter to all those outcasts who spent their childhoods wishing they were from another country.

Jason Schwartzman stars as Max Fischer, an underachieving academic who compensates for his poor classroom performance at Rushmore prep school by involving himself with every club on campus. He gets expelled anyway, just as he's falling in love with a teacher, a beautiful widow named Rosemary Cross (Olivia Williams). Cross resists his advances, and Max takes solace in a new friendship with the depressed, enervated Herman Blume (Bill Murray). Then Herman meets Rosemary and falls in love with her as well. She reciprocates, and Max gets upset. That's when things get complicated.

The story of a teenager falling for an older woman isn't new to film, but *Rushmore* uses it as a jumping-off point for a brilliant character study, a look at middle-aged despair, and the cartoon absurdity of Max's oversized ambition. Bill Murray's performance here helped set the course for his career revitalization as "hipster on the decline," and Williams has rarely been more luminescent, but the movie belongs to Schwartzman, who plays the pint-sized Max as an indomitable force of nature, someone whose willpower and passion are enough to conquer logic, good taste, and anything else that gets in his way. He's not always likable, but he's never less than fascinating, and anyone who's ever felt like reality would be significantly improved if it would just fall in line with her vision will find it easy to relate.

There is an arch distance from the real world that runs through *Rushmore*, a self-aware intelligence that responds to the world in the same way Max Fischer adapts films for the stage: through a series of whimsically constructed set pieces, where artifice and sincerity are rough equivalents. As Wes Anderson's career continued, this distance increased. His third film, **The Royal Tenenbaums** (2001), takes this distance a few steps further. While *Rushmore* used Max's working-class barber father to provide a contrast to the insular world of its titular academy, *Tenenbaums* dives head-first into a whimsical tale of wealthy intellectuals and their assorted despairs. Gene Hackman stars as the gruff patriarch of the Tenenbaums, a family of child prodigies who grow into depressed adults. It's a film that embraces its own world without question, and if you find it difficult to relate to precocious playwrights, tennis stars, and the intellectual elite, well, that's your lookout.

One of the main themes of *Tenenbaums*— the notion of adults perpetually reaching for the success of their younger selves—is the key to Anderson's next film, **The Life Aquatic with Steve Zissou** (2004). Bill Murray, who had a small role in *Tenenbaums*, takes the lead here as Zissou, a Jacque Cousteau-like ocean explorer past his prime, still struggling to hold on to the old magic. When a friend is killed by a Jaguar shark, Zissou sets out to find revenge, bringing along his faithful crew, a son (Owen Wilson), and a pregnant reporter (Cate Blanchett). Zissou is selfish, arrogant, and needy, and, much like the film itself, he can be difficult to like. But at heart he's simply a boy who refuses to do the adult thing and grow up. Anderson doesn't soften the character, but the writer/director has a clear sympathy for all manner of misfits who grasp life in the face of death, however childish that grasp may be.

This perspective is even more apparent in **The Darjeeling Limited** (2007). Jason Schwartzman, Adrien Brody, and Owen Wilson star as three brothers who are taking a train through India on a spiritual quest. The trio last saw each other at their father's funeral a year previous, and relationships between them are strained. *Limited* drew criticism in some quarters for its treatment of India as a fantasyland where white Americans can find themselves, but the movie is less about a country than it is about the promise of escape, and the way family bonds, perpetually elastic, snap into place again and again.

What is all of this to the Pythonite, one might ask. Even if one doesn't buy into Anderson's particular aesthetic, all his films are funny, wonderful to look at, with great music and sly performances. And they share with Monty Python a persistent immaturity, a refusal to settle into the accepted path of stolid middle age. Anderson's first animated feature (stop-motion), ***Fantastic Mr. Fox*** (2009), may be his most Pythonesque yet. George Clooney voices the title character, a former chicken-stealer who retires to a life of quiet desperation when his wife (Meryl Streep) gets pregnant with their first child (eventually, Schwartzman). But the old life calls to him, and soon he's back to his old tricks, earning the wrath of the most-feared farmers in the county. If *Rushmore* is a grown-up movie that yearns for childhood, *Fox* is a children's movie that acknowledges that there may be a few worthwhile aspects to being an adult after all. Pythonites will appreciate the dry tone, the great songs, and the understanding that responsibility doesn't take away the desire to, every once in a while, behave like a wild animal.

Monty Python never shied away from risk in their work. That was a big part of what made them so successful—*Flying Circus* mixed classic sketch comedy with innovative new techniques and an eagerness to rebel against convention. As a screenwriter, Charlie Kaufman knows the value of risk. His first film, ***Being John Malkovich*** (1999), has a core concept so bizarre it's hard to imagine an audience willing to sustain its belief long enough to follow the idea through an entire movie. But instead of playing it safe, Kaufman piles oddity on top of oddity, and the resulting dark comedy is a successful commentary on celebrity worship, unrequited love, and how much we all wish we could be someone else.

Craig Schwartz (John Cusack) is an out-of-work puppeteer who finds a job at LesterCorp, located on floor 7 1/2 of the Mertin

Flemmer Building in New York City. Depressed by a world that refuses to recognize the brilliance of his artistry, Craig attempts to start an affair with Maxine (Catherine Keener), an acerbic co-worker largely indifferent to his advances. But Craig has just the way to win her heart: a secret door discovered behind a file cabinet on 7 1/2 that serves as a portal into the mind of John Malkovich (John Malkovich). Anyone who goes through that door winds up inside Malkovich's head for fifteen minutes, seeing through his eyes and feeling what he feels. Along with Maxine, Craig starts a business charging people for use of the door, but Craig's wife (Cameron Diaz) also has eyes for Craig's new love, and there are others with more nefarious intentions for that portal...

The performances in *Malkovich* are great across the board, with Malkovich in particular giving a standout performance as his "real" self. *Malkovich* is Spike Jonze's first time directing a feature film, after having made a name for himself in music videos, and his straightforward, somewhat grim take on the film's fantasy elements helps sell the absurdity of it all. Really, though, the movie succeeds because of Kaufman's brilliant script, which treats the strangest of concepts with a deadly seriousness, with hilarious (and oddly moving) results.

If *Malkovich* has a flaw, it's that the movie can feel a little hollow; at times, the characters seem to be less living their lives then existing inside an experiment designed to see how they react to strange stimuli. Kaufman and Jonze fixed this problem in their next collaboration, 2002's **Adaptation**. When Kaufman set about adapting Susan Orlean's 1998 nonfiction book *The Orchid Thief*, he had trouble finding a way to bring the unstructured narrative to the screen. So he wrote a screenplay that took the basics of Orlean's book (most notably, the author's relationship with the titular character, John Laroche), and combined it with his own struggles to adapt the material.

The resulting picture should be massively self-indulgent and tediously meta. Instead, it's a fantastic, beautiful examination of how people change their lives to survive, and how the need to be unique can often be as damaging as the urge to conform. Nicolas Cage does double duty as an on-screen Kaufman, as well as Kaufman's twin brother Donald, and Meryl Streep appears as Orlean herself, who becomes entranced with Chris Cooper's roguish Laroche. Pythonites would be well advised to check out both *Malkovich* and *Adaptation* for examples of modern comedy at its smartest and most daring. And if they like what they see, they may also enjoy Kaufman's other films: the uneven but still worthwhile **Human Nature** (2001), the heartbreaking romantic fantasy **Eternal Sunshine of the Spotless Mind** (2004), and Kaufman's directorial debut, **Synecdoche, New York** (2008).

Modern mainstream American comedy tends to be a little lazy. Either you've got the low-key affability of the movies of Judd Apatow (*The 40-Year-Old Virgin, Knocked Up*) or the more frenetic hypermasculinity of something like *The Hangover*—both have their charms, but the devout Pythonite may not be satisfied with Apatow's laid-back rhythms, or with the more aggressive, mechanical action-comedy style. For a Python fan who wants to get a taste of mainstream comedy in the States, but wants to ease in with a movie that's at least in spitting distance of *Flying Circus*, Will Ferrell's **Anchorman: The Legend of Ron Burgundy** (2004) is a fairly safe bet. While the movie suffers from some of the gag redundancy that's typical of American comedy nowadays (which uses repetition without escalation), it's odd enough to stand out, as well as giving Ferrell one of his best big-screen roles.

It's the 1970s, and the local news anchorman is king. Ron Burgundy (Ferrell) is the head anchor of San Diego's most popular evening news program, and along with his team (Paul Rudd, Steve Carell, David Koechner), he rules his town like a clearly enunciating god. But times are changing, and one day Veronica Corningstone (Christina Applegate), an ambitious reporter with an eye to busting open the male-dominated world of reading words off a teleprompter and smiling with assurance, joins the Channel 4 news division. Burgundy feels his position of dominance is threatened, and to complicate matters further, he thinks he may be falling in love with this beautiful blonde firebrand.

Anchorman could theoretically be played straight (or straighter, anyway) as a conventional romantic comedy, as the unknowing sexism of Burgundy and his friends is gradually thawed by the light of open-mindedness and the possibility of romance. Thankfully, Ferrell and director and cowriter Adam McKay go a different route. One of the biggest jokes of *Anchorman* is that everything in it is ridiculous, even the parts that, in a more traditional movie, wouldn't be; the audience isn't supposed to take Burgundy and Corningstone's burgeoning love any more seriously than the surprisingly deadly battle royal between rival news teams, or Burgundy's taste for jazz flute. It's a silly, silly movie, and while it could arguably do with a little tightening, that silliness makes up for a lot, following in the grand Python tradition of taking the piss out of just about anything.

Remember the Gumby sketches from *Flying Circus*? No, it's nothing to do with that green slab of clay who liked jumping into books— "Gumby" to Monty Python (and their fans) meant a certain kind of moron, one who dressed in a familiar costume (suspenders, mustache, sweater vest, rolled-up trousers, kerchief on head) and spoke in a loud, doltish voice while doing loud, doltish things. It's not a bad bit; the joke seemed to be as much about the obviousness of the caricature of idiocy as it was about the idiocy itself. The Gumbys were oafs, prone to violence, shouting, and shouting while they did violence. Which is funny enough, especially in small doses. But imagine the Gumby was a representative of the world population: not an exaggerated spoof of fools, but an accurate measure of the current state of fooldom. And then imagine that the Gumbys and their ilk dominated society and controlled the government. It's a scary thought, and one that makes Mike Judge's 2006 movie ***Idiocracy*** as unsettling as it is funny.

Luke Wilson stars as Corporal Joe Bauers, a nice guy selected by the Army for a hibernation experiment due to his average IQ (100) and, well, general averageness. A prostitute named Rita (Maya Rudolph) is also selected for the experiment, which puts Joe and Rita inside a hibernation chamber to sleep for a year. Something goes wrong with the process, and instead of sleeping a year, the two are kept in storage until they wake up five hundred years into the future. They find the world a substantially changed place. As explained in the movie's opening sequence, the process of natural selection doesn't favor the intelligent, and given that the more educated are choosing to opt out of having children, while the less educated procreate with wild abandon, in the five hundred years since Joe and Rita knew America, the country has gotten substantially dumber. Farmers try to water crops with energy drinks, the most popular movie in America is a fart joke, and anyone who uses grammatically correct English in conversation is accused of "talking like a fag."

Idiocracy's script, by Judge and Ethan Coen, plays up the ridiculous aspects of a future full of morons, and Judge's direction goes for a light tone throughout, but there's no denying the creepiness of an entire species laid low by its inexorable march to stupidity. In concept, the movie plays like the worst fears of anyone who's ever struggled to explain the value of reading to a stranger, and if it weren't for Judge's clear affection for the morons he depicts, *Idiocracy* could easily have become overly strident. Instead, it's a funny, generally goofy look at an America that seems more and more possible with each passing year. *Idiocracy* has its weaker moments, and the ending doesn't quite live up to the movie's best scenes, but it's still worth a look for any Pythonite who ever dreamed of looking out his window and seeing Gumbys, Gumbys everywhere.

In **In the Loop,** Armando Iannucci's 2009 political satire, language is the weapon, and vulgarity is the blade. As Malcolm Tucker, the Prime Minister of the United Kingdom's Director of Communications, Peter Capaldi is a veritable Jack the Ripper of filth who terrorizes the lives of his minions and fellow government employees with elaborately verbose curses and vaguely veiled threats of physical violence. *Loop* (a spin off of the BBC series *The Thick of It*, also starring Capaldi) is the story of how words lead to war, but the only shots fired on-screen are sentences. Basically, it's a terribly funny horror movie in which no one dies, but a few careers implode, and a few noble intentions are strangled in the name of expediency.

One morning, during an otherwise innocuous interview, a low-level politician in British government (Tom Hollander) makes the mistake of saying he thinks war in the Middle East is "unforesee-able." This upsets certain other powerful Brits, who are working with forces in the American government to make that war a reality, and Tucker swoops in to try and control the damage. Hollander continues to dig himself in deeper, taking a trip to the States, where he gets involved with American officials on the pro- and anti- sides of the war cause. Whichever direction he goes, he manages to make things worse in a farce where the only victory is making sure the egg lands on the other guy's face.

Monty Python were never much for cursing. The group certainly didn't shy away from the occasional vulgar aside, but swears in *Flying Circus* or their various films were shocks because they were exceptions to the rule. But Python and *Loop* agree on the power of language, and both find immense humor and rhetorical power in floods of eloquent abuse. The absurdity of language is a regular theme in Python sketches, and in *Loop*, part of the joke are the elaborate, outrageous insults concocted and let fly in the halls of the powerful. What's funny and horrifying about *Loop* is the way adults who should know better often make decisions based more on petty vengeance and a desire for status than on anything approaching reason. The boundless cynicism would be depressing if it weren't so painfully hilarious.

Suicide bombers are terrifying; once people are so convinced of the rightness of their beliefs that they're willing to sacrifice their own lives to murder others for the sake of those beliefs, they've passed beyond a place of rational thought. It's hard to talk to somebody so adamant in faith that the regular rules don't apply, and it's even harder to relate to that level of commitment, ideology, and madness. And it's not exactly a funny topic, either. Dark comedy is great and all, and who doesn't like a good laugh at death and all that, but making jokes about a real and present danger is tricky business, especially one that's been as politicized and mythologized as Osama bin Laden's crusade against the Western world. Odds are, any gags about the difficulty of getting the right bomb fuel without raising suspicion, or the awful sensitivity of homemade explosives, will get buried under misguided attempts at political correctness and forced sentiment.

Amazingly enough, director Chris Morris's **Four Lions** (2010) gets laughs from just those gags, and plenty more besides, following the misadventures of a group of would-be suicide bombers living in Sheffield, England. The secret is to treat the young Muslim men, heroes in their own minds, without commentary or overt criticism, which humanizes them without forgiving their behavior. Riz Ahmed plays Omar, the leader of the group, a family man whose loving wife supports his plans for violence; Kayvan Novak is Waj, Omar's not-terribly-bright pal; Nigel Lindsay is Barry, a white convert to Islam who makes up for his lack of intelligence with a temper and fervency; and Adeel Akhtar, whose attempts to train crows as potential bombers goes as well as one would expect. The cast settles easily into familiar comedic rhythms as Omar struggles to maintain coherency with a group that can't agree on much of anything, let alone pull together for the most important (and last) mission of their lives.

What's so impressive is that *Four Lions* never shies away from its central premise, and manages to be terribly funny right up until things get deadly serious. And even then, there are laughs to be found. (One of the film's best gags has the group transporting bombs in broad daylight across a suburban street, trying to be both nonchalant and incredibly careful with the material.) In a world where any mention of "jihad" or "Al Qaeda" or even "Muslim" is bound to stir the sort of controversy that prohibits thinking, *Lions* would be impressive just for telling its story without overt judgment. The fact that the script (by Morris, Jesse Armstrong, Sam Bain, and Simon Blackwell) and the cast are so routinely gut-busting (no pun intended) is icing on the cake. Pythonites will appreciate the deft handling of sensitive material and the unsettling reminder that the people who commit inhuman acts tend to be human after all.

George Carlin in the 1970s. (Photofest)

6

AND NOW FOR SOMETHING COMPLETELY DIFFERENT . . .

While Monty Python was opening the Flying Circus to pay their tribute to the mighty *Goon Show*, back in America, four men were following the Goons' lead to their own ends. **The Firesign Theater**, made up of Phil Austin, Peter Bergman, David Ossman, and Philip Proctor, began life in the '60s doing live radio programs, but their legacy today is best represented through their comedy albums, starting with 1968's ***Waiting for the Electrician or Someone Like Him***. The group is still active today. *Firesign* extrapolates outward from the Goons' absurdism; their work is characterized by stream-of-consciousness delivery, with lines and sounds suggesting a variety of settings and comedic ideas. It can be a bit much, especially considering how often the group depends on pop culture references that seem obscure today, but their best work captures the Goons' charm and adds a subversive, singularly American edge.

Firesign's two best albums are two of its earliest: ***How Can You Be in Two Places At Once When You're Not Anywhere At All*** (1969) and ***Don't Crush That Dwarf, Hand Me the Pliers*** (1970). *Places* is split neatly into two halves, represented as sides on the original record release. On Side A (the side that gives the album its title), an ad for the world's most perfect recreational vehicle segues into riffs on then familiar commercial figures, the Marx Brothers, and W. C. Fields, before building to an extended assault on American greed and exceptionalism. On Side B, "The Further Adventures of Nick Danger," the group does one of its longest sustained parodies, a jokey take on a private detective mystery that makes Firesign's debt to *Goon* very clear.

Don't Crush That Dwarf mixes the rapid-fire strangeness of Side A of *Places* with the occasional long-form parody (like a riff on '50s teen drama and Archie comics) to tell the five ages of George Leroy Tirebiter. It's a less accessible recording than "Nick Danger," which is probably the best starting place for those unfamiliar with the group, but arguably more heartfelt. While the *Goons* and Monty Python worked to find the humor in the surreal, Firesign Theater strove to find the surreal in humor. The result are challenging, often bizarre, and, at their best, mesmerizing.

Douglas Adams was a friend to Monty Python. He worked briefly with the troupe, getting a writer's credit on one *Flying Circus* (a rare honor) and appearing briefly on two episodes of the show. It's only natural, then, to hope that the work Adams is best known for might also be of interest to Pythonites. Thankfully, that hope is well rewarded in Adams' two best-loved series: **The Hitchhiker's Guide to the Galaxy**, a five-novel trilogy; and the Dirk Gently novels, **Dirk Gently's Holistic Detective Agency** (1987) and **The Long Dark Tea-Time of the Soul** (1988).

The Hitchhiker's Guide to the Galaxy started life as a series for BBC radio in 1978, but it's best known in its novel form, originally published in 1979. It tells the story of Arthur Dent, an average Englishman with the good fortune to be friends with an alien named Ford Prefect. Arthur isn't aware of his luck until the day that the Vogons destroy the Earth to make way for an interstellar bypass, vaporizing everyone on the planet except Ford and Arthur, who hitch a ride on their ship. Soon after, Arthur and Ford hook up with Zaphod Beeblebrox, the two-headed former President of the Galaxy, and his current girlfriend, Trillian, an Earth woman Arthur once tried to pick up at a party.

Hitchhiker's spoofs a number of science fiction conventions (like the super-fast spaceship engine, here rendered as "the Improbability Drive," or the mundanity of the destruction of Earth) and maintains a whimsically sincere tone throughout, as Arthur haplessly struggles to make sense of a galaxy that proves to be just as mad as life on Earth. Adams would continue Arthur's adventures with ***The Restaurant at the End of the Universe*** (1980), ***Life, the Universe and Everything*** (1982), ***So Long and Thanks for All the Fish*** (1984), and ***Mostly Harmless*** (1992). Though uneven, the series has enough great gags and likable characters to be worth the time. It's a somewhat gentler, if still deeply cynical, sort of humor than the Pythons normally engaged in, although even the Pythons might shy away from the nihilistic conclusion of *Harmless*. (Adams died in 2001, but Eoin Colfer wrote a sixth entry in the series, *And Another Thing . . .*, which was published in 2008.)

There are fewer Dirk Gently novels, and the series isn't as well known as the *Hitchhiker's* books, but *Detective Agency* and *Tea-Time* are both supremely clever. Dirk Gently is one of Adams's greatest fictional creations, a metaphysical private eye who solves mysteries that no one else can. In *Detective Agency*, he starts on a case of a missing cat, investigates a murder, and helps save the human race from extinction, and in *Tea-Time*, he deals with some grumpy Norse gods. The Gently books don't have as clear a satirical target as *Hitchhiker's*, but they are clear evidence of Adams' comic genius and knack for convoluted, playful plotting.

For fans of lighthearted spoofs more interested in fantasy fiction than sci-fi, there's Terry Pratchett, whose Discworld series takes sword-and-sorcery conventions to task in much the same way that *Hitchhiker's* mocked the space opera genre. But Pratchett's work shows a deeper affection for his characters than Adams's, as well as a thematic concern with basic decency and the power of belief. Anyone interested in getting an idea of Pratchett's work could do worse than picking up ***Good Omens*** (1990). Cowritten with Neil Gaiman, the novel is a comic version of a modern-day apocalypse, following a young Antichrist who may not quite want to bring about the end of the world, and the angel and demon best friends who aren't as invested in maintaining their respective roles as they properly should be.

Omens is a great introduction to Pratchett's major interests, treating its various warring figures from religious tradition with a genial humanism at odds with their mythic origins. For Pythonites who enjoyed *Omens* and would like a good entry point into the Discworld series, there's ***Small Gods*** (1992). The Discworld series has a number of recurring characters and storylines, and a basic continuity that follows form the series' first novel, *The Colour of Magic*. *Gods* is largely standalone (in that it exists in the Discworld universe, but doesn't feature any of the series' major characters, apart from Death), and also one of Pratchett's best novels.

A passionate, inspiring fable about the relationship between gods and men, and how kindness and respect are the only faith that truly matters, *Gods* follows Brutha, a devout novice of the Omnian faith. One day the great god Om attempts to manifest Himself before his followers, but the faith has become so corrupted over the years that the god arrives as a turtle whom only Brutha can see and hear. The interplay between the desperately arrogant god and his plodding, sincere disciple is as spiritually rewarding as it is comically effective, although *Gods* never becomes didactic or overtly preachy. Rather, it's all good common sense: even gods could stand to learn a thing or two about being humble, and even the smallest man can be great. Both Adams and Pratchett carry on the Python spirit with their own unique brands of humanism, and both make for excellent reading for devout Pythonites.

It comes down to a matter of perspective. There are plenty of reasons to be a fan of Monty Python—"they're funny" is a big one—but what turns someone into a Pythonite is a feeling of sympathy with the group's take on life. To Cleese, Idle, Palin, Jones, and Gilliam, the world is a strange place and people make it stranger, and the only way to respond to all the strangeness is to try and increase it tenfold. For anyone who sees things this way, *Flying Circus* is as much an oasis as it is a comedy series, offering a place where one's own peculiar ideas are the rule, not the exception. Really, though, great comedy (and great art) comes from a strong perspective regardless if that perspective is one that audiences share. The more distinct and honest a joke is, the better it lands. To that end, here are a few stand-up comics that Pythonites may want to look into.

Richard Pryor told the truth the only way he seemed to know how: fearlessly. A sometime drug addict who once set himself on fire while freebasing cocaine, Pryor had what one might call a life rich with incident, and his genius lay in recognizing this and bringing those incidents to the stage in an act that helped set the modern stand-up tone of intimacy, fearlessness, and audience empathy. Pryor appeared in a number of movies, some decent, some less so (anyone only familiar with the performer from his work in *Superman III* (1983) might be understandably amazed that he was a comic genius), and he did some television work as well; the comedian also cowrote the script of *Blazing Saddles* with Mel Brooks and was set to star in the movie, but the studio insurance company refused to underwrite him. His best work was on the stage, in stand-up routines that brought together the disparate threads of a complicated, frustrated, passionate persona into something like art. In his albums and his concert movies, Pryor is friendly and open and takes absolutely no shit from anyone, like a man who finds his sanity in only one place on Earth, and then resolves to share it. Every other comedian on this short list would name Pryor as an influence, and for good reason—he set the standard for laughing with a straight face.

George Carlin was a contemporary of Pryor's, and would occasionally mention the other stand-up in his own act; in ***Carlin at Carnegie*** (1983), Carlin compares his two heart attacks to Pryor's one heart attack and lighting himself on fire. But while Carlin was willing to talk about his own life on stage, his comedy was less about the confession, and more about commenting on the absurdities of day-to-day life. Which, admittedly, is what a lot of comedy is based on, but Carlin's observations are part of an overall philosophy that sets him above the rest. To Carlin, reality was always a few screws short of a thing that needed more screws, and his job was to make sure no one ever forgot just how weird it is that some words are considered dangerous, while others are not. Carlin had his own substance-abuse problems, and while he was better served by the film industry than Pryor, the stand-up's best work is still found on stage, in routines that brush up against nihilism without completely giving in to despair. Where Pryor told stories from his own life and struggles, connecting with his audience through his directness and willingness to reveal himself at his worst, Carlin's appeal is broader, calling attention to the discrepancies and paradoxes that we all share.

Both Pryor and Carlin are dead, Pryor in 2005, Carlin in 2008, but while both men died too soon for their fans and loved ones, they still had a fair amount of material to leave behind. (This holds true even though the disease multiple sclerosis, diagnosed in 1986, limited Pryor's productivity in the last two decades of his life.) The same can't really be said of **Bill Hicks,** a stand-up punk pioneer who died in 1994 at the age of thirty-two. It could be that the performer's premature death (of pancreatic cancer) has helped strengthen his legacy over the years, putting him in the lofty annals of any cutting-edge artist who died before he had a chance to fade away; but whether that's true or not, the work that does remain is powerful and entertaining enough on its own to justify the attention. Pryor confessed, Carlin poked, and Hicks harangued, using his routines and jokes as a way to tear into bad government, the commercialization of rock music, and anything else that caught his attention.

In his weaker moments, when the stand-up was facing disinterested audiences and struggling with his own demons, Hicks could sometimes be too hectoring, a scream thrown against a wall by a man infuriated by architecture. But Hicks's best performances, like those recorded on the albums *Dangerous* (1990), *Relentless* (1992), and the posthumous *Arizona Bay* (1997) and *Rant in E-Minor* (1997), are funny, humane, and full of compassion for the challenges of trying to hold on to your sense of humor in the face of society seemingly intent on breaking down every individual, piece by piece. Like all the comedians in this list, Hicks's biggest contribution to the art form is his persona—in this case, a class clown who can't help being shocked by what the other guys get away with.

Patton Oswalt has made a career out of making it look easy. A stand-up who trades in pop culture poetry, geek identity, self-laceration, and compassion, Oswalt has passed through sitcom obscurity to stand today as the King of Nerdery, a wholly uncomfortable sage more likely to mock his own failings than preach. Arguably the key to Oswalt's success (in addition to all the great joke writing and gift for delivery) is his vulnerability. On stage, Oswalt seems comfortable and at ease with himself, and he doesn't take crap from anyone, but unlike Pryor or the others, Oswalt doesn't come across as a rebel or a sage. As a King, he makes a humble ruler, constantly drawing attention to his struggles with exercise, his doubts about his ability to raise his daughter, and his own outcast status in a world that favors shallow good looks over, well, just about everything. But Oswalt never plays for pity, and his riffs on his physique and general social awkwardness make both sound more normal than so-called normalcy. Oswalt's routines are literate, peppered with obscure references (which mock their own obscurity), and open without being overly grim, and his moments of social commentary are more plain-spoken common sense than fiery rhetoric.

Oswalt has done good work in film (including Pixar's **Ratatouille** (2007), where he provided the voice for Remy, a food-loving rat; and *Big Fan* (2009), where he starred as a sports enthusiast whose world is upended by a chance encounter with one of his heroes), and he's written an essay collection, **Zombie Spaceship Wasteland** (2011), that mixes memoir with parody for moderate success. But his stand-up remains vital. His best album, **222** (2003), is the closest thing to seeing him live there is, outside of actually seeing him live—a two-hour unedited recording of a night of stand-up at the 40 Watt Club in Athens, Georgia. The jokes don't always land, but the jokes are only part of Oswalt's appeal; it's the personality that brings the audiences in, and that comes through in every fumbling minute.

Listening to **Maria Bamford**'s album *Unwanted Thoughts Syndrome* (2009), one thing becomes immediately clear: Maria Bamford has a funny voice. Listen to it further, and that funny voice becomes one of *several* funny voices. Bamford runs through routines about competing with her sister, applying for a job, listening to inordinately soothing radio DJs, and working as a temporary Bjoran for a mall-touring *Star Trek* show, and through each bit, her tones match the material: shrill when necessary, sometimes strident, other times mellow and seductive. It's a bravura performance, and Bamford's most immediately identifiable trait as a comedian, but while her vocal modulations are impressive, they wouldn't be worth near as much if the material she delivers weren't equally as strong.

Bamford uses her skills to heighten already-clever jokes about the way passion can warp our lives, and how the more disproportionately intense a person becomes over a cause, the more ridiculous the person and the cause quickly become. Bamford isn't afraid to mock herself (the album opens with her attempts to prank call her parents as the baby Jesus, and in the competition against her hyper-productive sister, Bamford is more than willing to admit her own sloth), but for the most part, the album stays above personal confession, sticking in the silly, surreal world of overly militant pug-dog trainers and ex-Deadhead art counselors. Her humor is based more on character than punch line, but it never sags the way character humor can. *Syndrome*'s finale has Bamford discussing her struggles with obsessive-compulsive disorder, and the moment of seriousness (which, to Bamford's credit, isn't really serious at all) helps put the whole album in a slightly different context: here's another performer who mocks insanity to keep herself sane, and the world is better for it.

Then there's **Paul F. Tompkins.** A natty dresser who spent the most of the '90s doing background work on television shows like *Mr. Show* and *Tenacious D*, Tompkins has been coming into his own in the past few years as a cultural critic and man about town, hosting his own podcast, ***The Pod F. Tompkast***, and running a popular Twitter feed. But if all this technology is a bit confusing to the average consumer, fear not—the wit and wisdom of PFT can be conveniently downloaded or purchased at your local record store in the form of his 2009 album, ***Freak Wharf***.

Wharf opens with a few tracks' worth of Tompkins riffing in front of a live audience, and while the improvised bits aren't as consistent as the album's scripted material, they show a mind working overtime to pull at stray threads and silliness. Easily the least open about his personal life of any of the comics listed here,

Tompkins finds a potentially rich subject—like, say, the overly emotional words of new fathers, or the smashed penny machine at amusement parks—and mines that subject for every possible laugh it contains. Tompkins isn't particularly edgy, and his social commentary doesn't amount to much more than "What the hell, right? Jeez," but he's funny, smart, and knows how to work a bit for all it's worth. Which may make him the closest to Monty Python, in the end. But, as with the other comics mentioned here, the key to Tompkins's rising success is his commitment to his own particular view of the world. A comedian, or a sketch troupe, without perspective, is like an old knock-knock joke—easy to deliver, but not saying anything that hasn't been said a thousand times before.

The dog doesn't talk. That's the key to the joke right there—Gromit, the dog, will raise his eyes, shrug his shoulders, or glare, but he never, ever talks. Because, of course, dogs *can't* talk. Not even dogs made of clay who can run bakeries, fly to the moon, and fight off serial killers. Gromit's incredibly competency makes language almost unnecessary, but for one thing: Gromit's hapless, accident-prone owner, Wallace. Voiced by Peter Sallis, Wallace is a well-meaning inventor whose overcomplicated inventions sometimes make life difficult for him and his faithful canine companion. Wallace makes big plans, falls in love, and gets entangled in nefarious plots against him that he never notices until just before it's too late. It's up to Gromit to keep Wallace safe from his own foolishness and anyone who means him harm. This would be a lot easier to manage if Gromit could only explain himself.

Creator and animator Nick Park released the first Wallace & Gromit half-hour short in 1989. ***A Grand Day Out*** has our heroes running out of cheese before a holiday. Wallace comes to the only possible conclusion: the moon is made out of cheese, so he'll build a rocket and they'll fly to the moon and have all the cheese they want. The stop-motion clay animation in *Grand Day Out* isn't as advanced as it would be in later shorts, but it's still effective, and the story (cowritten by Steven Rushton) is charming and handily establishes the character of its two leads. The next short, ***The Wrong Trousers*** (1993), is considerably more ambitious. The story, cowritten with Bob Baker, has Wallace and Gromit menaced by a felonious penguin. In 1995's ***A Close Shave,*** the duo is up against a psychotic dog and some sheep in peril. Wallace and Gromit hit the big screen with the feature-length ***The Curse of the Were-Rabbit*** (2005), a spoof on Hammer horror movies that had the heroes dealing with a horrible shape-changing curse and a potential new love for Wallace. And in their last outing to date, 2008's short ***A Matter of Loaf and Death***, it's up to Gromit to show Wallace that his new ladylove might not be as well-intentioned as he'd like to believe.

One of the main sources of Wallace and Gromit's appeal is its solidity. The stop-motion clay animation fits in well with Wallace's Goldbergian inventions, complicated methods for getting seemingly simple results. The shorts and the film seem to have an endless supply of whimsy, full of clever sight gags, terrific slapstick set pieces, and a sweetness that never feels forced or sloppily sentimental. Python understood, as all great comedians understand, that timing is key in humor, and the work of Park, in each of Gromit's strained expressions and double-takes, shows a keen grasp on the rhythms of humor, wringing the most wry laughter out of each second. But then, that's not really a surprise. Given how the stop-motion technique requires artists to break down moments to their smallest segments, Park has had ample opportunity for study. Lucky for us, he's clearly made the most of it.

Is there anything sillier than a superhero? Probably, but at the very least, putting on a fancy costume before running around a city at night punching strangers isn't the act of a rational person. These days, hardly a month goes by without movie theaters showing a new iteration of the now tired tale: a young man gets some new power thrust upon him by fate or radioactivity, and then, after a bit of soul searching and maybe some first-base action with the hottie next door, that young man decides it's his job to stand up to evil and get really angsty about doing so. Given the amount of money riding on all these potential franchise starters, it's not surprising that few of them are willing to be open about the inherent foolishness of their central concept, but as an audience member, it's hard not to get sick of all the seriousness. Thankfully, we have **The Tick** (1994–1996) to bridge the gap for us—given that Monty Python is no longer available.

Ben Edlund first created the Tick in 1986 as a mascot for New England Comics; the character wouldn't make his full comic debut until 1988. The character got his own animated series in 1994, and hadn't changed much from his printed origins. A largely invulnerable, certified insane muscle-bound oaf who dressed up in blue spandex and shouts "Spoon!" at crime before he hits it, the Tick is something of a mystery, but his lack of clear origin is part of his appeal. With his sidekick, the perpetually petrified Arthur, the Tick battles ninjas, chair-headed super-villains set on defacing the moon with their signature, and pint-sized evil geniuses who have glass bowls where their skulls should be. To aid them in their quest, there's the heroic American Maid (a Wonder Woman / Captain America goof), Die Fledermaus (a Batman spoof), and Sewer Urchin, a *Rain Man*-esque take on Aquaman.

The animated series is full of nods that will appeal to comic book fans, but the concept is broad enough for anyone to appreciate. The characters are well drawn (pun intended), covering a mix of superhero cliché and straight surrealism. The Tick himself perfectly encapsulates both the standard superhero's ridiculousness and his boundless appeal: an eternally optimistic, good-natured buffoon, the blue bomber is at once stupid to the extreme (when Arthur temporarily quits his sidekicking duties, the Tick adopts a small wooden puppet in his place), and so warmhearted and cheerful it's impossible not to love him. A live-action series based on the character, also called **The Tick,** aired for nine episodes in 2001. It's not terrible (and Patrick Warburton does a fine job in the title role), but the Tick, Arthur, and the rest are best suited to animation and the page, where they're simply the logical extension of brightly colored heroes and crazy evil schemes. Pythonites should enjoy the parody and the great one-liners.

. . .

One of Steve Martin's greatest gifts as a performer is his ability to make effort seem like part of the joke. His signature stand-up routine, with all its seemingly tossed-off stupidity, was clearly the result of concentration, study, and hard work, and the audience's awareness of that work helps provide context. That wasn't a moron on stage, it was a smart man pretending he was a moron— much as the Pythons, even at their most foolish, were extraordinarily clever. Martin retired from stand-up years ago, and in his 2007 memoir, ***Born Standing Up***, he explains why. The short book explains a lot of things, actually, serving as a spotty autobiography from the notoriously shy star, as well as a history of his act on stage, how and why he decided to be a comic, and why he decided to walk away from one of the most profitable stand-up acts in history.

Martin's clear, crisp style makes *Born Standing Up* a very fast read. The book is even easier to enjoy in audio format, with the author himself serving as narrator, turning the prose into, essentially, a four-hour-long monologue and polite manifesto about the art of making comedy. The book isn't as in-depth about Martin's personal life as a more traditional biography might be, but it's a great window into the performer's philosophy, his goals, and the rise of an act from small stages in near-empty rooms to stadiums full of screaming fans. For anyone interested in the process behind the jokes, *Born Standing Up* is essential reading, revealing how no moment, no matter how seemingly insignificant, happens without a plan. Great silliness comes only with great concentration, something Steve Martin (and the Pythons) had in spades.

Humor in gaming is very, very tricky. Timing is a key part of successful comedy, and video games can only dictate their own rhythms to a certain extent. The player is always going to have a significant amount of control over how the piece runs, and that means gags that look great on the page get stretched out past recognition, or repeated so often that the words lose meaning. Plus, while it's reasonable to assume that a Pythonite will enjoy movies, television shows, and books, gaming is a bit more specialized. There have been a handful of computer games released based on Monty Python material, but by and large these are no more than pleasant time-wasters. Anyone looking for the height of video game humor and design will be more interested in checking out **Portal** (2007) and **Portal 2** (2011), by the Valve Corporation.

The premise of both *Portal* games is straightforward enough. You play Chell, a test subject for the Aperture company. A malevolent artificial intelligence known as GLaDOS (Genetic Lifeform and Disk Operating System) runs you through a series of increasingly difficult and life-threatening puzzles that revolve around your use of the portal gun. The gun is the game's main premise: a handheld device that allows the user to shoot an orange hole into one wall, and a blue hole into another. Go in the orange hole, you come out the blue hole. It's as simple as that, but the concept leads to often astonishingly complex puzzle design. Using a first-person perspective (the gamer sees through Chell's eyes), the *Portal* series sends players through fiendishly difficult test rooms involving complicated jumps, lasers, and eerily friendly gun robots who chirrup hello right before they fire. The further Chell gets, the clearer it becomes that GLaDOS's bland pleasantries cover for a more sinister agenda. The cake is a lie—and so is everything else.

GLaDOS's trickery makes for a more intense gaming experience, but it's also part of what makes these two games of interest to Python fans. *Portal* and *Portal 2* are terribly funny games, and they get around the problem of timing by getting laughs as much out of an overall aesthetic as out of individual lines. The contrast between GLaDOS's politeness and her murderous intentions helps drive the first *Portal*, adding a sinister undercurrent to the bland concrete walls and well-lit environments. *Portal 2* brings in Stephen Merchant (cowriter and codirector of *The Office*) as an in-over-his-head robot drone, and J.K. Simmons (*Burn After Reading*) as the voice of the long-dead company president, to create an environment of lethal incompetence where ego and hubris create deadly, hilarious results. Video games may not be for everyone, but these two are worth a look for the curious.

From "The Ministry of Silly Walks." (BBC-TV/Photofest © BBC-TV)

APPENDIX A:
FAMOUS MONTY PYTHON QUOTES
AND HOW TO USE THEM

Monty Python's Flying Circus

1. "A nod's as good as a wink to a blind bat, say no more, say no more!"

Originally appeared in: "How to Recognise Different Types of Trees from Quite a Long Way Away"

Context: A single man eagerly peppers a married man with insinuations, desperate for knowledge about sex.

When to Use It: In awkward social situations as an attempt to break the ice; during prolonged police interrogations; after inadvertently stumbling across an exchange of information between spies, in order to convince them not to shoot you; if you think the person you're talking to has had intercourse recently, and you'd like information about the experience.

When Not to Use It: If you are in conversation with an actual blind bat.

2. "Are you an encyclopedia salesman?"

Originally appeared in: "Man's Crisis of Identity in the Latter Half of the Twentieth Century"

Context: A housewife trying to determine if the man at her door is an encyclopedia salesman. She would rather he was a burglar.

When to Use It: When trying to determine a stranger's occupation; in order to indicate doubt in the truthfulness of another's statements, i.e., "You expect me to believe that? Are you an encyclopedia salesman?"

When Not to Use It: The annual Conference of Almanac and Concordance Peddlers.

3. "This is a late parrot! It's a stiff! Bereft of life, it rests in peace! If you hadn't nailed it to the perch, it would be pushing up the daisies! It's rung down the curtain and joined the choir invisible. This is an ex-parrot!"
Originally appeared in: "Full Frontal Nudity"
Context: A man bought a parrot at a pet shop, only to find it was already deceased. He would like a refund.
When to Use It: To identify oneself as a Python fan to other Python fans; when faced with a rude or inept sales clerk; in an effort to lighten up a beloved relative's funeral.
When Not to Use It: To comfort a bereaved pirate.

4. "I'm a lumberjack and I'm okay / I sleep all night and I work all day!"
Originally appeared in: "The Ant, an Introduction"
Context: A lumberjack sings about the joy of cutting down trees, being manly, and wearing women's underwear.
When to Use It: Open mike nights; confessing one's true sexual orientation and/or tendency towards transvestism to one's parents; road trips through the Canadian wilderness.
When Not to Use It: The Republican National Convention.

5. "He was perfectly normal in every way! Except … inasmuch as he thought he was being followed by a giant hedgehog named Spiny Norman."
Originally appeared in: "Face the Press"
Context: A female impersonator gives some insight into the murderous psychology of Dinsdale Piranha.
When to Use It: When trying to describe a strange friend whose eccentricities can't really be put into words; when talking with giant hedgehogs, just to let them know you're on their side; to get an enemy committed to an insane asylum through the power of reverse psychology.

When Not to Use It: In the presence of a mentally deranged criminal who might assume you're making fun of him.

6. "*Nobody* expects the Spanish Inquisition!"
Originally appeared in: "The Spanish Inquisition"
Context: For once, it's pretty much what you'd expect—upon hearing the line "Nobody expects the Spanish Inquisition," a trio of Inquisitors burst onto the scene.
When to Use It: At surprise parties; when questioned about an error at work ("How was I supposed to know there'd be a rainstorm? *Nobody* expected the Spanish Inquisition!"); trying to explaining to your guests why you didn't get enough soda and hot dogs for everyone; as the concluding sentence of your closing remarks to a jury.
When Not to Use It: While defusing a bomb.

7. "It's just gone eight o'clock and time for the penguin on top of your television set to explode."
Originally appeared in: "How to Recognise Different Parts of the Body"
Context: A television announcer predicts the fate of a bird perched on a TV with great accuracy.
When to Use It: If you'd like to tell people what time it is, and want to lighten the mood with a joke; as a needlessly complicated metaphor describing the irrational state of modern network programming; to make sure the penguins know who's boss.
When Not to Use It: While defusing a bomb.

8. "I AM NOT A LOONY! Why should I be tarred with the epithet 'loony' merely because I have a pet halibut?"
Originally appeared in: "Scott of the Antarctic"
Context: A loony tries to buy a fish license for his pet halibut.
When to Use It: As an appeal to the common humanity of the psychologists at the asylum after your enemy has you committed there; at a rally for the rights of fish and the men who love them; to calm down anyone in earshot who have been made nervous by your persistent Monty Python quotes.

When Not to Use It: While speaking with a giant talking halibut.

9. "I DON'T LIKE SPAM!"

Originally appeared in: "Spam"

Context: A woman rejects a dinner option.

When to Use It: When you are unhappy about your meal; when you open up your e-mail program to find it full of advertisements for genital enlargement and letters from deposed African kings who need your bank account number to regain their lost fortune; to insult a generic or tedious entertainment product.

When Not to Use It: If you like spam.

10. "It's..."

Originally appeared in: The opening of nearly every episode of *Monty Python's Flying Circus*

Context: A hermit would like us to know that something is coming.

When to Use It: Before something arrives; after being poisoned or shot, to give your last few moments of life additional suspense; when you need to say "It is," but simply don't have time to get both syllables out.

When Not to Use It: While watching the opening of *Monty Python's Flying Circus.*

Monty Python and the Holy Grail

11. "It's not a question of where he grips it! It's a simple question of weight ratios! A five-ounce bird could not carry a one-pound coconut."

Context: A knight is questioning where King Arthur got the coconuts his squire is banging together to simulate the sound of trotting horses.

When to Use It: To point out that a situation has become untenably ridiculous; in order to change the subject quickly when you and your lover are interrupted by her husband; on the first day of physics class, to show the teacher you're on to his game.

When Not to Use It: After the apocalypse, when sparrows are a memory, and coconuts a dream of those wealthy in gasoline and airships.

12. "Bring out yer dead!"

Context: A man with a cart comes through town, collecting corpses.

When to Use It: When dropping by the morgue to pick up their recycling; while driving by the nursing home, to inspire heart attacks and passionate letters to the editor; to liven up funerals; to trick serial killers into revealing themselves in sketchier parts of town.

When Not to Use It: During a zombie attack.

13. "You can't expect to wield supreme power just 'cause some watery tart threw a sword at you!"

Context: A peasant is trying to explain to King Arthur the logistical and legal problems inherent in his rise to the throne.

When to Use It: When deposing the dictator of a banana republic (after making sure the dictator has been sufficiently restrained); when called on during a civics class that you haven't made any effort to study for; to give someone at a bar you're trying to hit on the impression that you're political.

When Not to Use It: Around anyone with actual power, and a temper.

14. "Well, she turned me into a newt!" "A newt?" "...I got better."

Context: Sir Percival is instructing ignorant townsfolk in the ways of witch-finding; one of the peasants claims to have a history with the witch.

When to Use It: After ending a relationship, to explain to friends why you thought it was time to move on; to justify to your health insurance provider why you switched doctors; to demonstrate to the pessimist that any circumstance, even forced shape-shifting, can be overcome with time.

When Not to Use It: If you are still a newt. (People can tell.)

15. "Your mother was a hamster and your father smelt of elderberries!"

Context: A French knight mocks King Arthur and his men.

When to Use It: In the buildup to a street fight, while you're trying to enrage your opponent with insults about his lineage and poor hygiene; to make an orphan appreciate the mystery of his past; to psych out your pets.

When Not to Use It: While arguing with a sibling.

16. "It's only a model."
Context: King Arthur's faithful squire, Patsy, doesn't understand the fuss everyone is making about the castle on the hill before them.
When to Use It: After Junior breaks a crucial piece while trying to glue together his airplane kit; whenever anyone gets overexcited about anything, just to show it's all pointless in the end, and you're better than them; to psych yourself up before your date with a Victoria's Secret employee.
When Not to Use It: When special effects guru Rick Baker unveils his latest work.

17. "The Knights Who Say Ni demand a sacrifice!"
Context: On his quest for the Holy Grail, King Arthur and his men come across a band of strange knights.
When to Use It: To let everyone in the area know you are about to annoy the heck out of them by shouting "Ni!" in a nasal whine for at least five minutes.
When Not to Use It: Around anyone who's armed.

18. "Who would cross the Bridge of Death must answer me these questions three, ere the other side he see."
Context: Arthur and his knights must face off against a power bridge guard.
When to Use It: If you're a bridge-guarding troll and you'd like to screw with some goats; before giving a pop quiz to a high school English class; if you just want to be a dick to someone trying to get inside the bathroom.
When Not to Use It: Around anyone who's armed.

Life of Brian

19. "I think it was 'Blessed are the cheesemakers'!"
Context: A man mishears Jesus's Sermon on the Mount.
When to Use It: To casually point out that someone may be misinterpreting holy writ; to draw attention to how easy it is to hear

what you want to hear; to impress a room of dairy professionals that you really are on their side.

When Not to Use It: Around the fervently lactose-intolerant.

20. "I'm not oppressing you, Stan. You haven't got a womb! Where's the fetus gonna gestate? You gonna keep it in a box?"

Context: A man argues with a fellow revolutionary about his demands for absurd rights.

When to Use It: While debating with anyone who doesn't realize how ridiculous he sounds; to lighten the mood during a feminist rally; as part of a pitch for a new horror movie, *Box Baby*.

When Not to Use It: Around a pregnant woman in labor.

21. "You lucky, lucky *bastard*."

Context: A prisoner is jealous of Brian's favorable treatment by the guards.

When to Use It: Whenever a friend gets a bit of jealousy-inducing good fortune; when your nemesis gets off a seemingly impossible shot, in the final seconds before your plans are completely destroyed; when your opponent draws a royal flush during the last hand of a World Championship Poker tournament.

When Not to Use It: Around thin-skinned orphans.

22. "Always look on the bright side of life."

Context: Brian has been crucified. He awaits a painful, agonizing death, and a fellow victim sings a song to cheer him up.

When to Use It: In times of great trauma or emotional hardship, or when you're just trying to score some points with cheap irony.

When Not to Use It: If you're dead.

APPENDIX B:
DO NOT ADJUST YOUR SET:
A LIST OF MUSTS FOR MONTY PYTHON ADDICTS

75 MOVIES A PYTHONITE MUST SEE

Adaptation
The Adventures of Baron Munchausen
Airplane!
Amazon Women on the Moon
An American Werewolf in London
Anchorman
Annie Hall
Barton Fink
Bedazzled
Being John Malkovich
Being There
The Big Lebowski
Blazing Saddles
Brain Candy
Brazil
Burn After Reading
A Clockwork Orange
The Darjeeling Limited
Dead Men Don't Wear Plaid
Dirty Rotten Scoundrels
Dr. Strangelove, or How I Learned to Stop Worrying and Love the Bomb
Duck Soup
Fantastic Mr. Fox
A Fish Called Wanda

The Fisher King
Four Lions
The General
Groundhog Day
A Hard Day's Night
Heathers
Help!
Hot Fuzz
The Hudsucker Proxy
Idiocracy
In the Loop
The Informant!
The Jerk
The Kentucky Fried Movie
Kind Hearts and Coronets
The Ladykillers (1955)
The Lavender Hill Mob
The Life Aquatic with Steve Zissou
The Man in the White Suit
The Man with Two Brains
Modern Times
The Mouse That Roared
The Muppet Movie
The Naked Gun
A Night at the Opera
O Brother, Where Art Thou?
Phantom of the Paradise
Raising Arizona
Ratatouille
Real Life
Repo Man
Rosencrantz and Guildenstern Are Dead
The Royal Tenenbaums
The Ruling Class
Rushmore
The Rutles

Schizopolis
Shaun of the Dead
Sherlock, Jr.
A Shot in the Dark
The Stunt Man
Synecdoche, New York
The Tall Guy
This Is Spinal Tap
Time Bandits
Top Secret
Twelve Monkeys
Waiting for Guffman
Wet Hot American Summer
Withnail and I
Young Frankenstein

50 TELEVISION SHOWS A PYTHONITE MUST WATCH

ASSSSCAT
The Avengers
The Ben Stiller Show
Big Train
A Bit of Fry & Laurie
Black Books
Blackadder
Chappelle's Show
Community
The Dana Carvey Show
Death Comes to Town
Doctor Who
Father Ted
Fawlty Towers
Futurama
Garth Marenghi's Darkplace
How to Irritate People
I'm Alan Partridge
The IT Crowd

It's Garry Shandling's Show
Jeeves and Wooster
The Kids in the Hall
Knowing Me Knowing You with Alan Partridge
The Larry Sanders Show
The League of Gentlemen
Louie
The Mighty Boosh
Mr. Show
The Muppet Show
Mystery Science Theater 3000
NewsRadio
Not Only ... But Also
The Office (BBC)
Party Down
Police Squad
The Prisoner
Red Dwarf
The Rocky & Bullwinkle Show
Saturday Night Live
SCTV
The Secret Policeman's Balls
The Simpsons
Spaced
The State
That Mitchell and Web Look
The Tick (animated)
Tim and Eric Awesome Show, Great Job!
Upright Citizens Brigade
The Venture Brothers
The Young Ones

AND 46 OTHER ODDITIES A PYTHONITE SHOULD CONSIDER

DOUGLAS ADAMS
Dirk Gently's Holistic Detective Agency
The Hitchhiker's Guide to the Galaxy
Life, the Universe, and Everything
The Long Dark Tea-Time of the Soul
Mostly Harmless
The Restaurant at the End of the Universe
So Long and Thanks for All the Fish

MARIA BAMFORD
Unwanted Thoughts Syndrome

ALAN BENNETT, PETER COOK, JONATHAN MILLER,
DUDLEY MOORE
Beyond the Fringe

GEORGE CARLIN
Carlin at Carnegie
It's Bad for Ya

GRAHAM CHAPMAN
Looks Like a Brown Trouser Job

LOUIS C.K.
Chewed Up
Hilarious
Shameless

THE FIRESIGN THEATER
Don't Crush That Dwarf, Hand Me the Pliers
*How Can You Be in Two Places At Once When You're Not
    Anywhere At All*

BILL HICKS
Arizona Bay
Dangerous
Rant in E-Minor
Relentless

STEVE MARTIN
Born Standing Up

SPIKE MILLIGAN, HARRY SECOMBE, PETER SELLERS
The Goon Show

BOB NEWHART
Behind the Button-Down Mind of Bob Newhart
The Bob Newhart Show
The Button-Down Mind of Bob Newhart
The Button-Down Mind Strikes Back
The Button-Down Mind on TV
Newhart
Something Like This… The Bob Newhart Anthology

PATTON OSWALT
222
Zombie Spaceship Wasteland

NICK PARK
A Close Shave
The Curse of the Were-Rabbit
A Grand Day Out
A Matter of Loaf and Death
The Wrong Trousers

TERRY PRATCHETT
Good Omens (with Neil Gaiman)
Small Gods

RICHARD PRYOR
The Anthology: 1968–1992
Richard Pryor: Live in Concert

CHARLES SCHULZ
Peanuts books

PAUL F. TOMPKINS
Freak Wharf
The Pod F. Tompkast

VALVE CORPORATION
Portal
Portal 2

INDEX